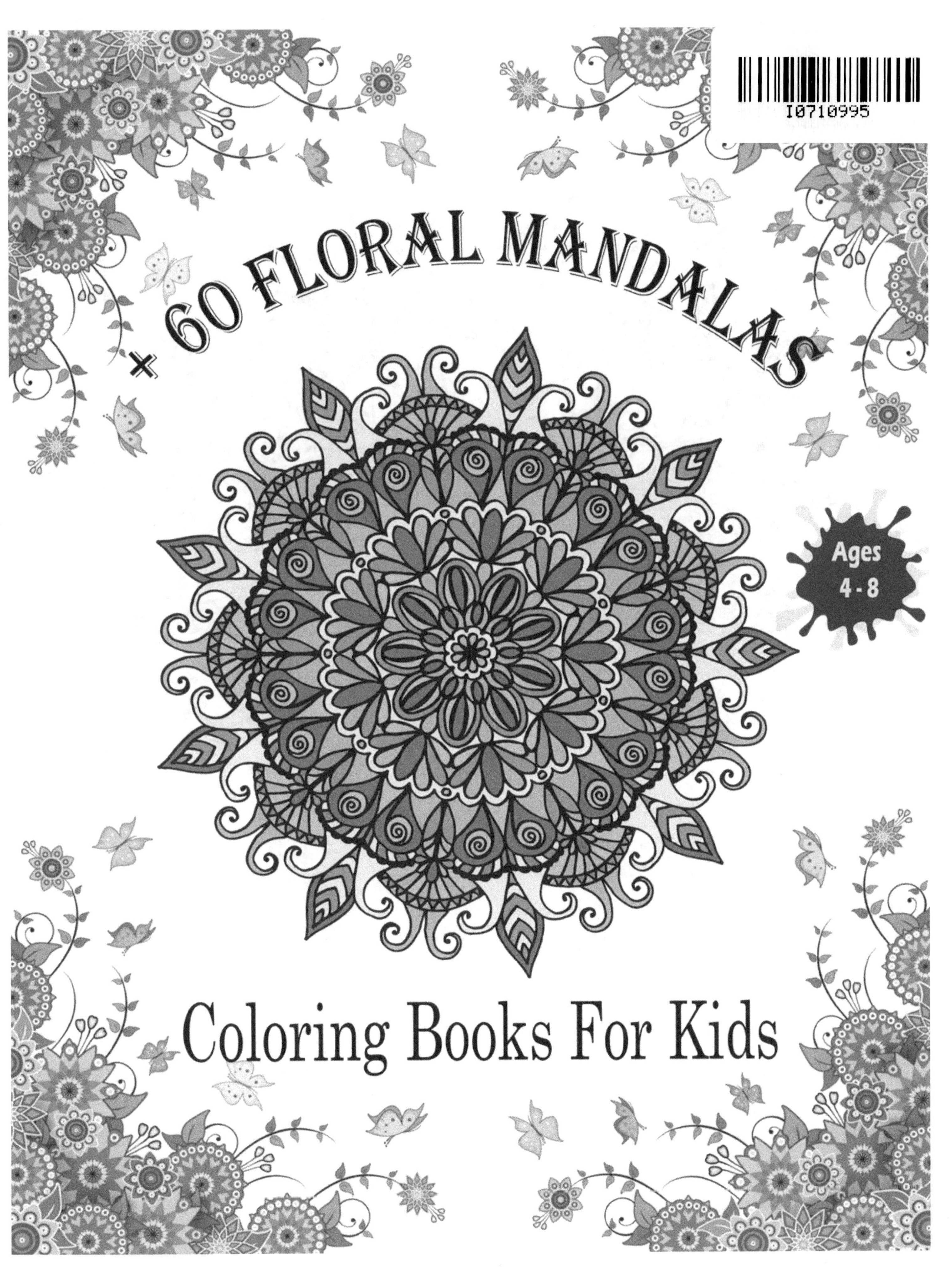

+ 60 FLORAL MANDALAS
Ages 4 - 8
Coloring Books For Kids
I0710995

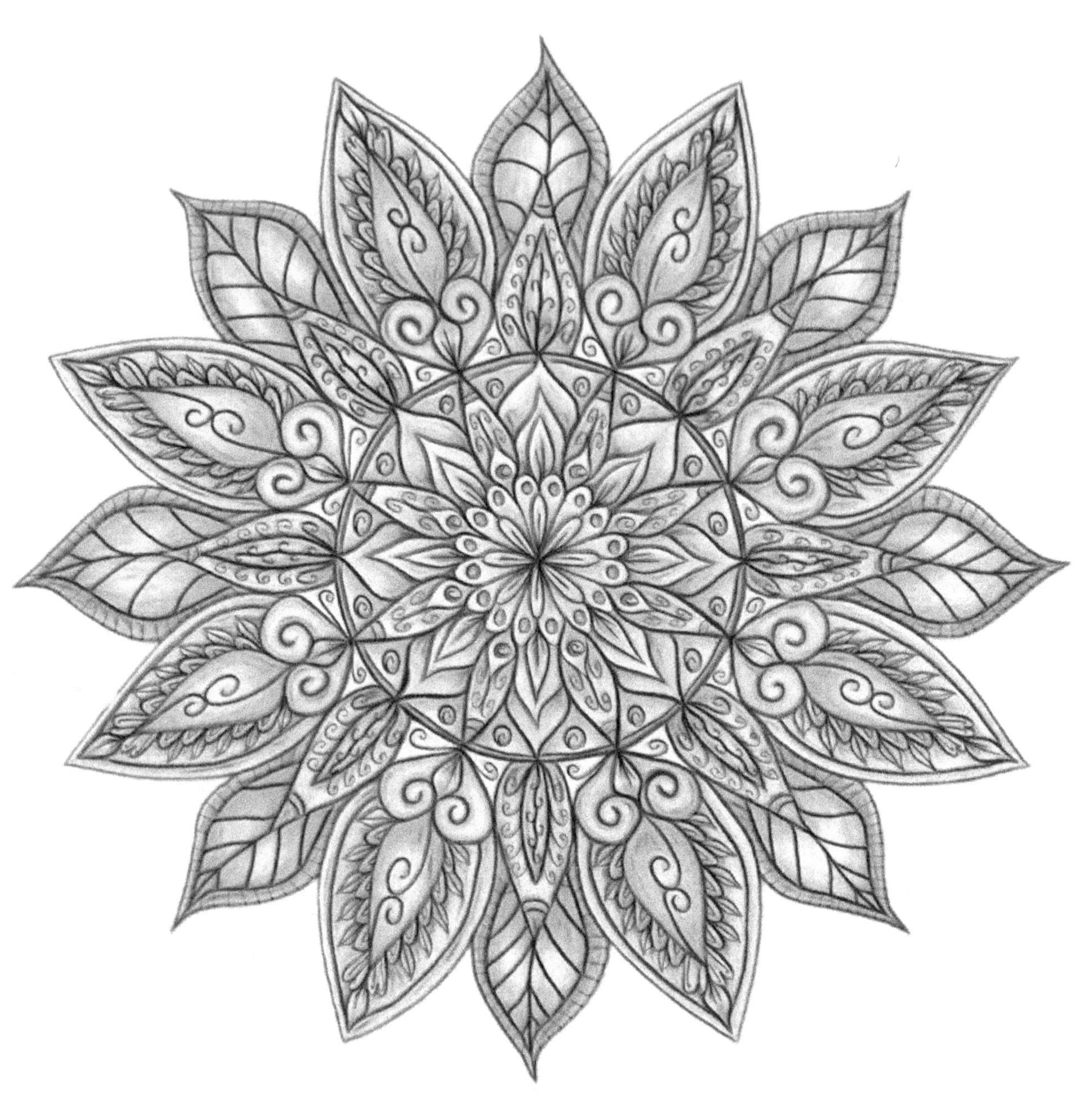

Copyright © 2020 By Jordi Publisher

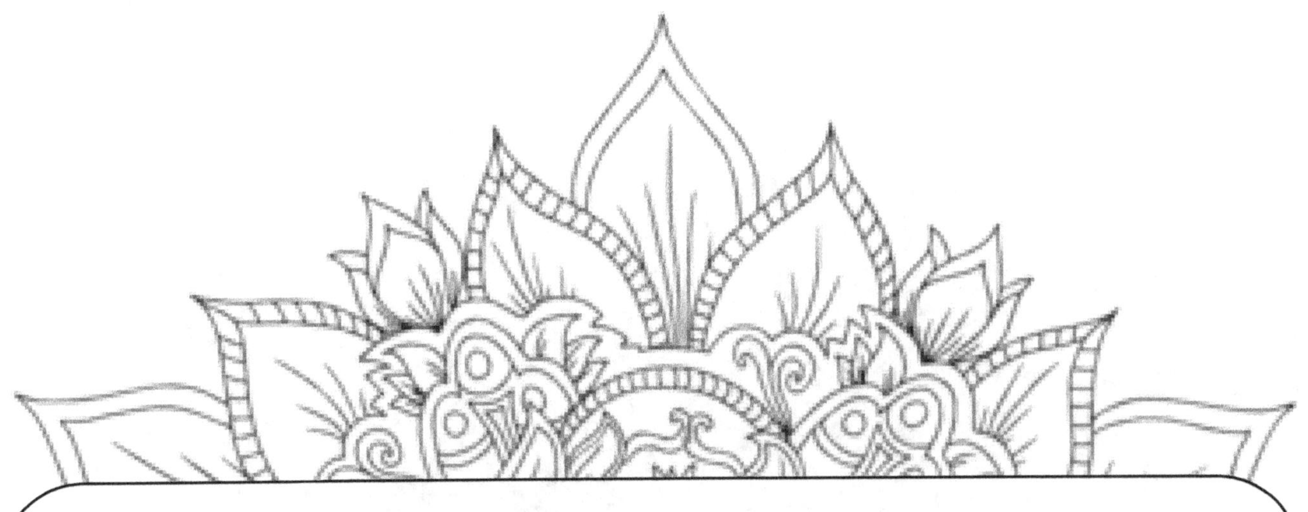

THIS BOOK BELONGS TO :

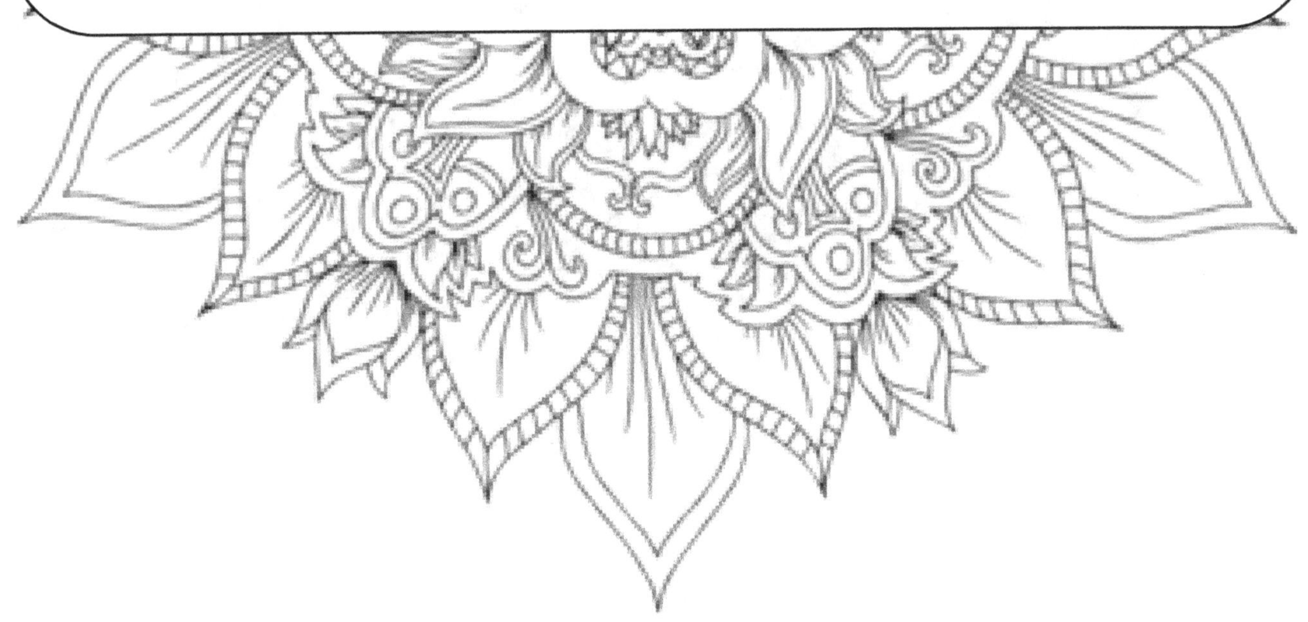

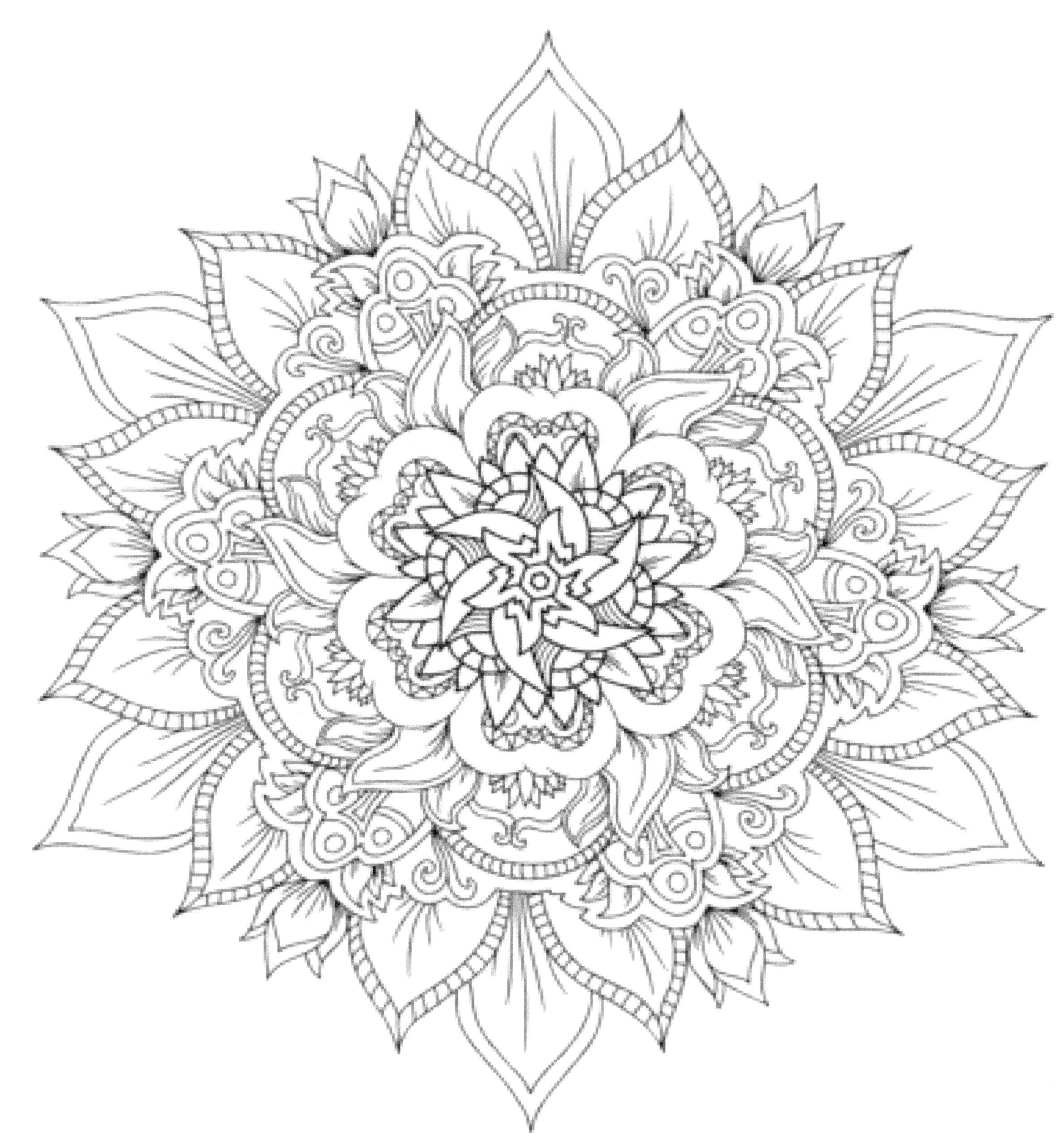

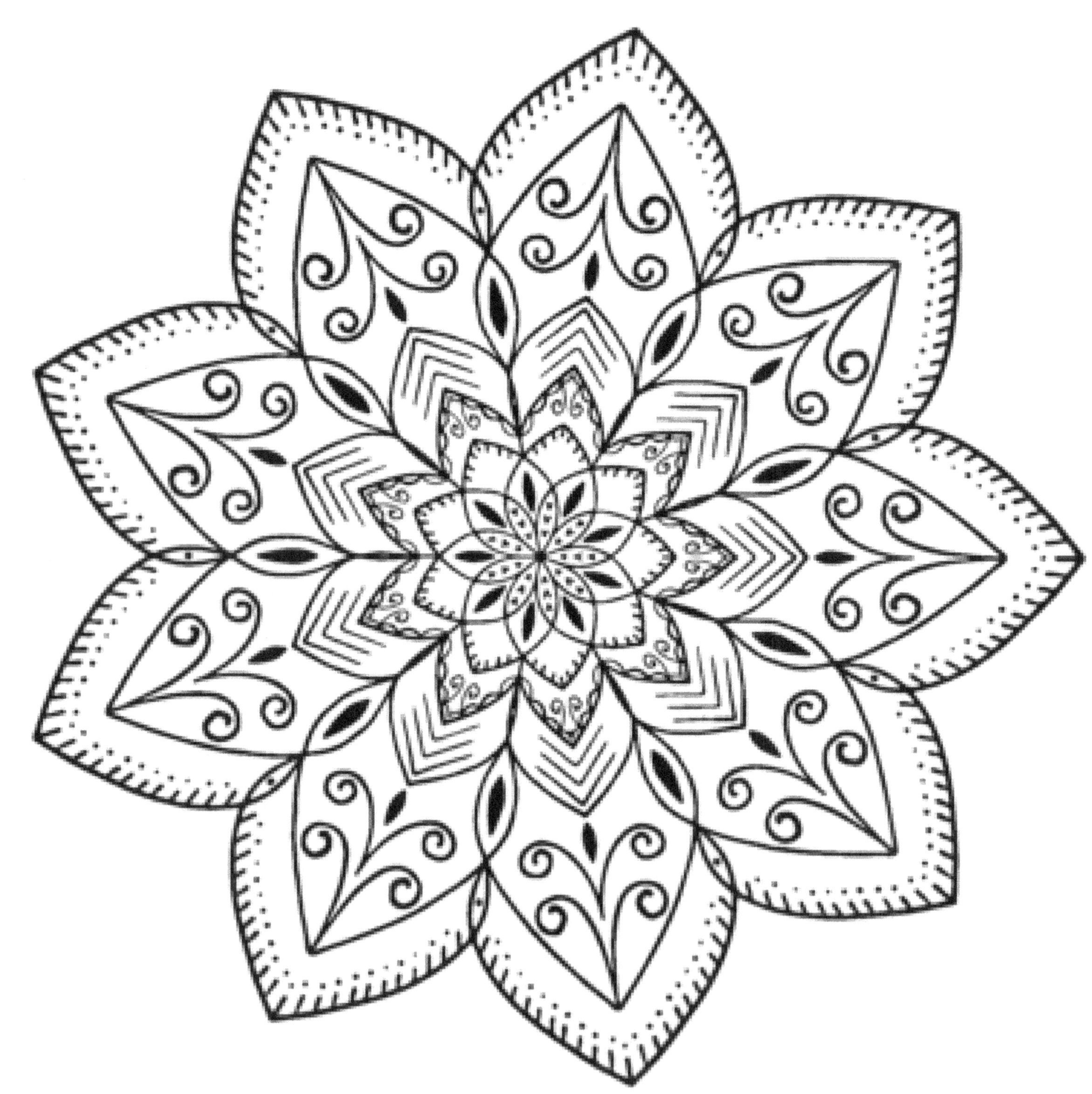

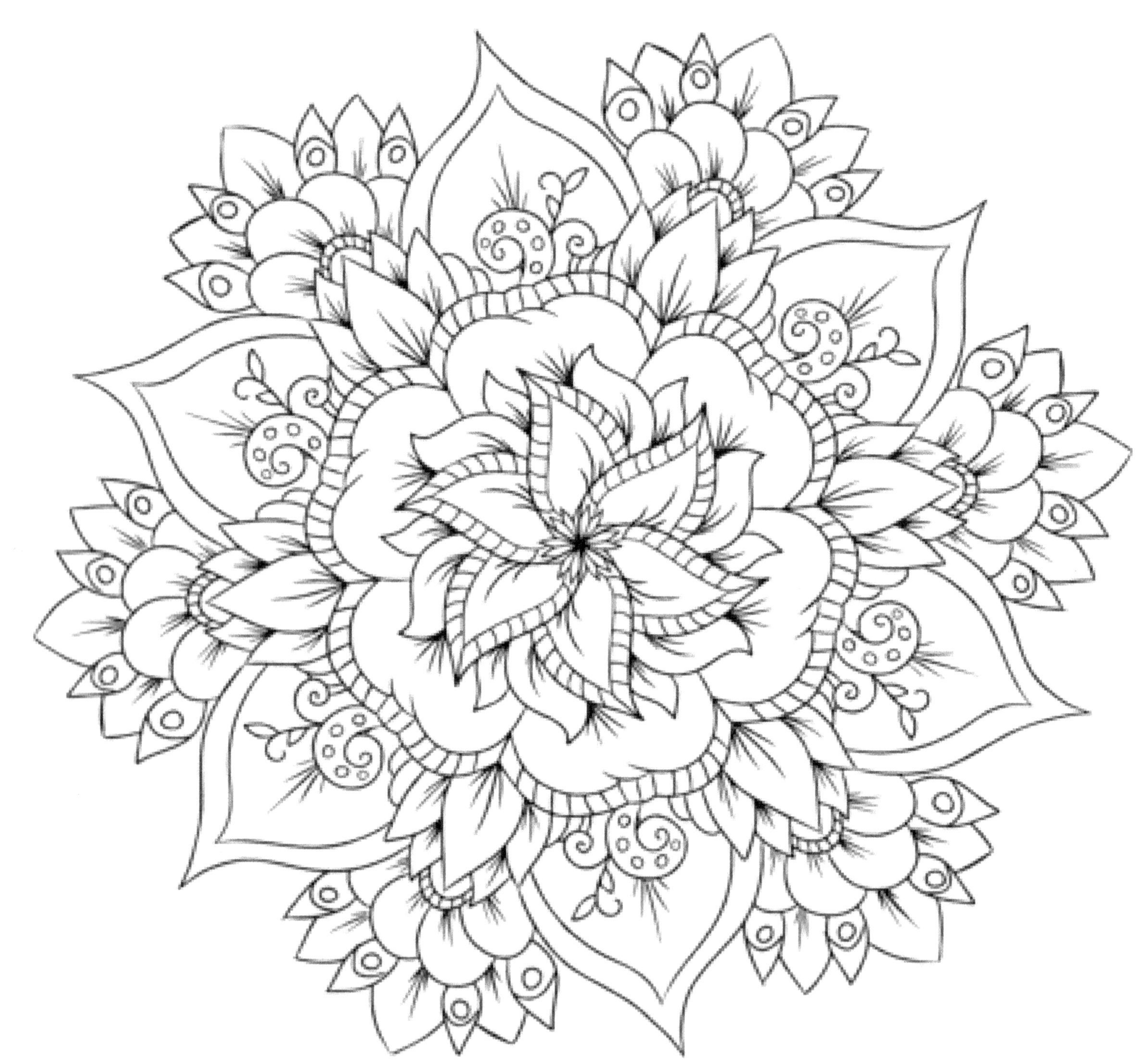

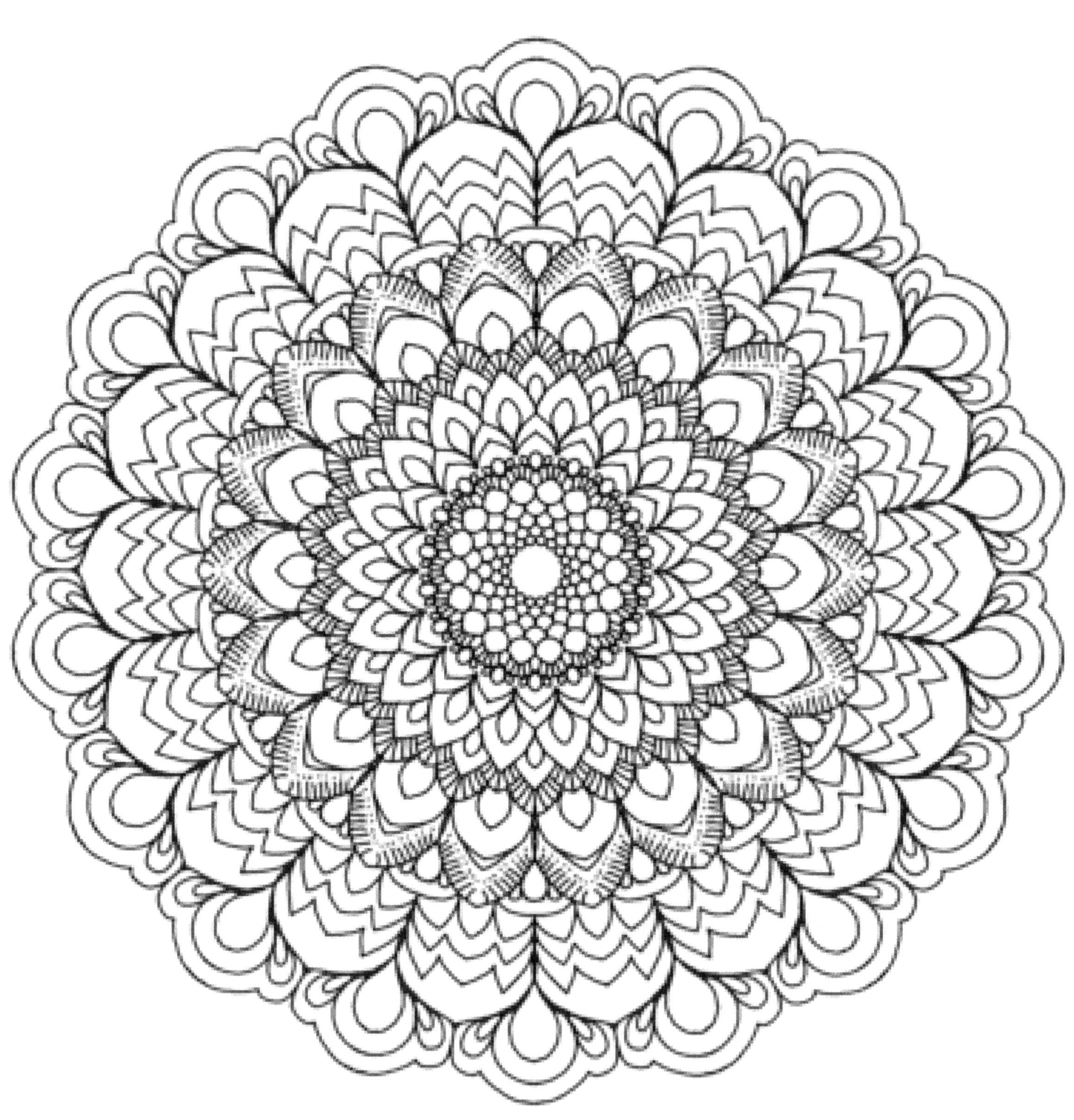

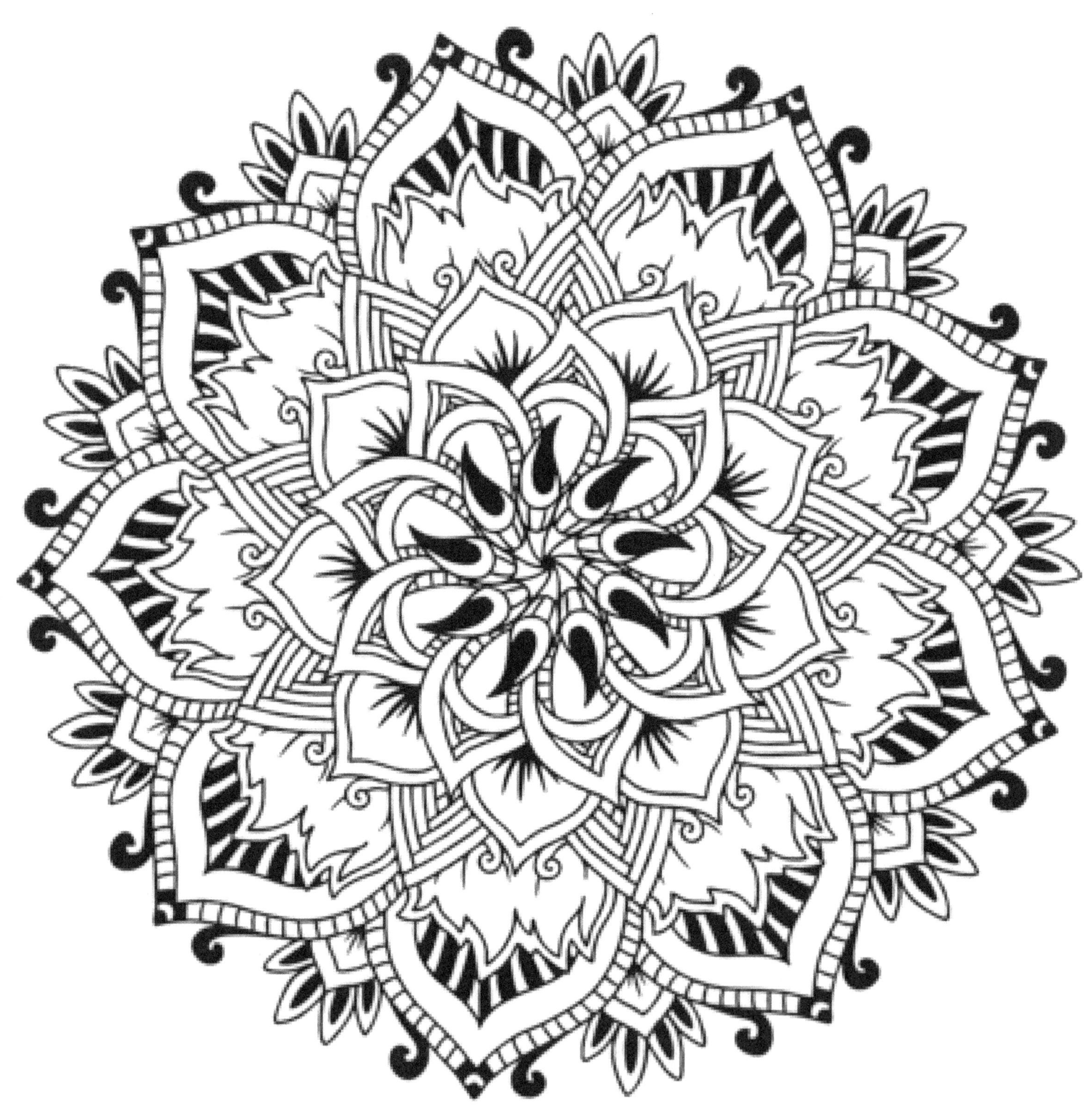

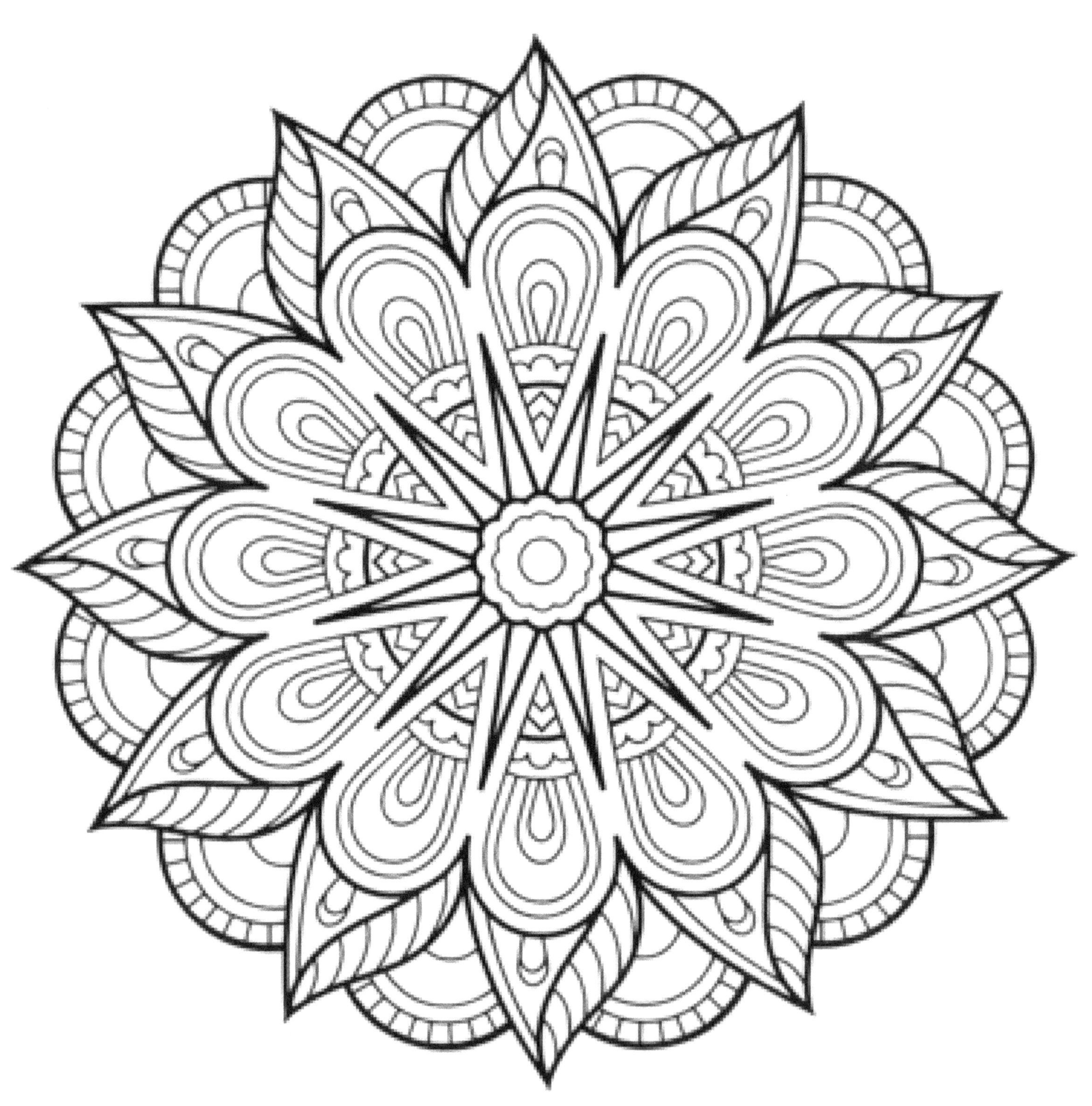

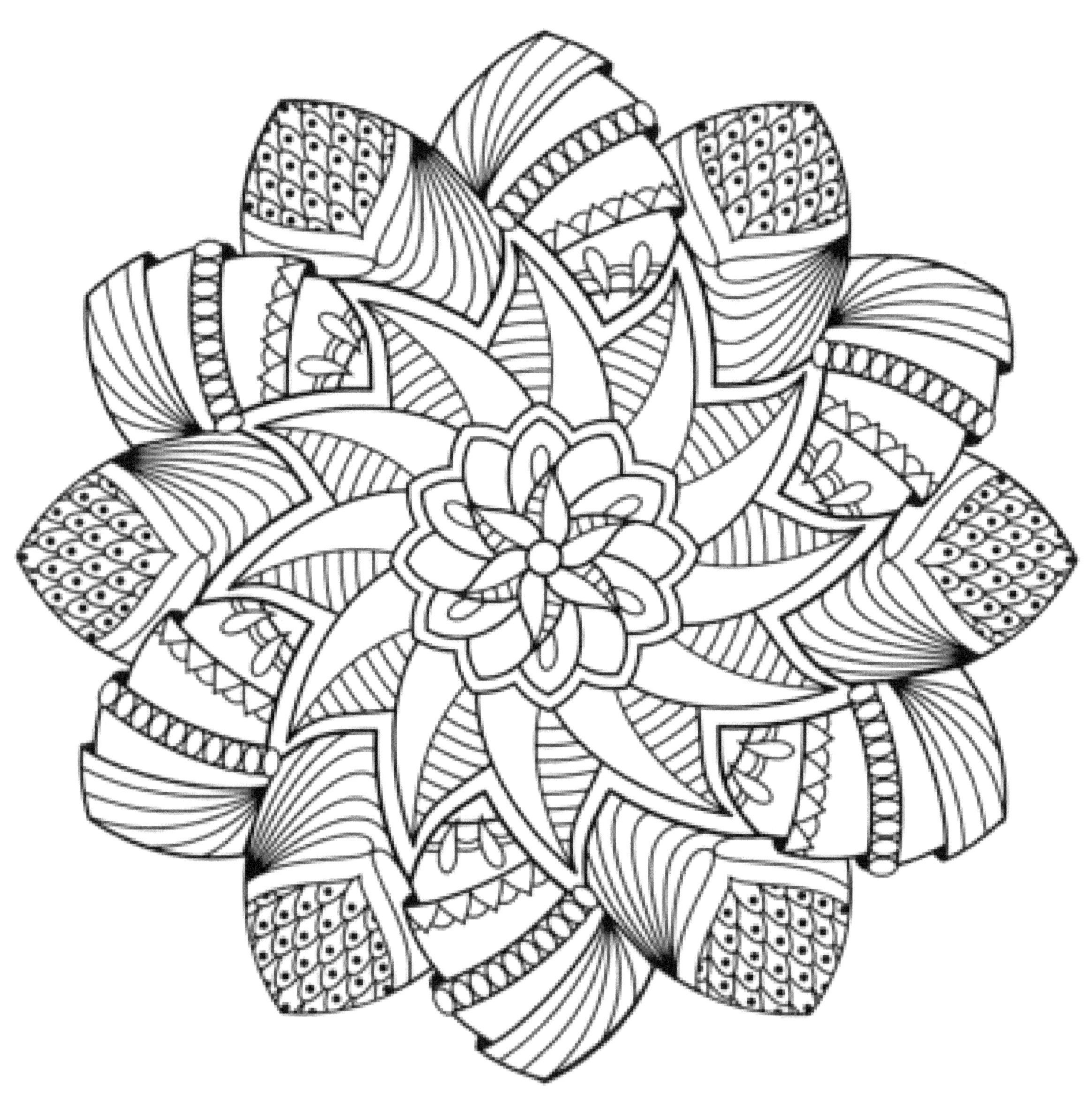

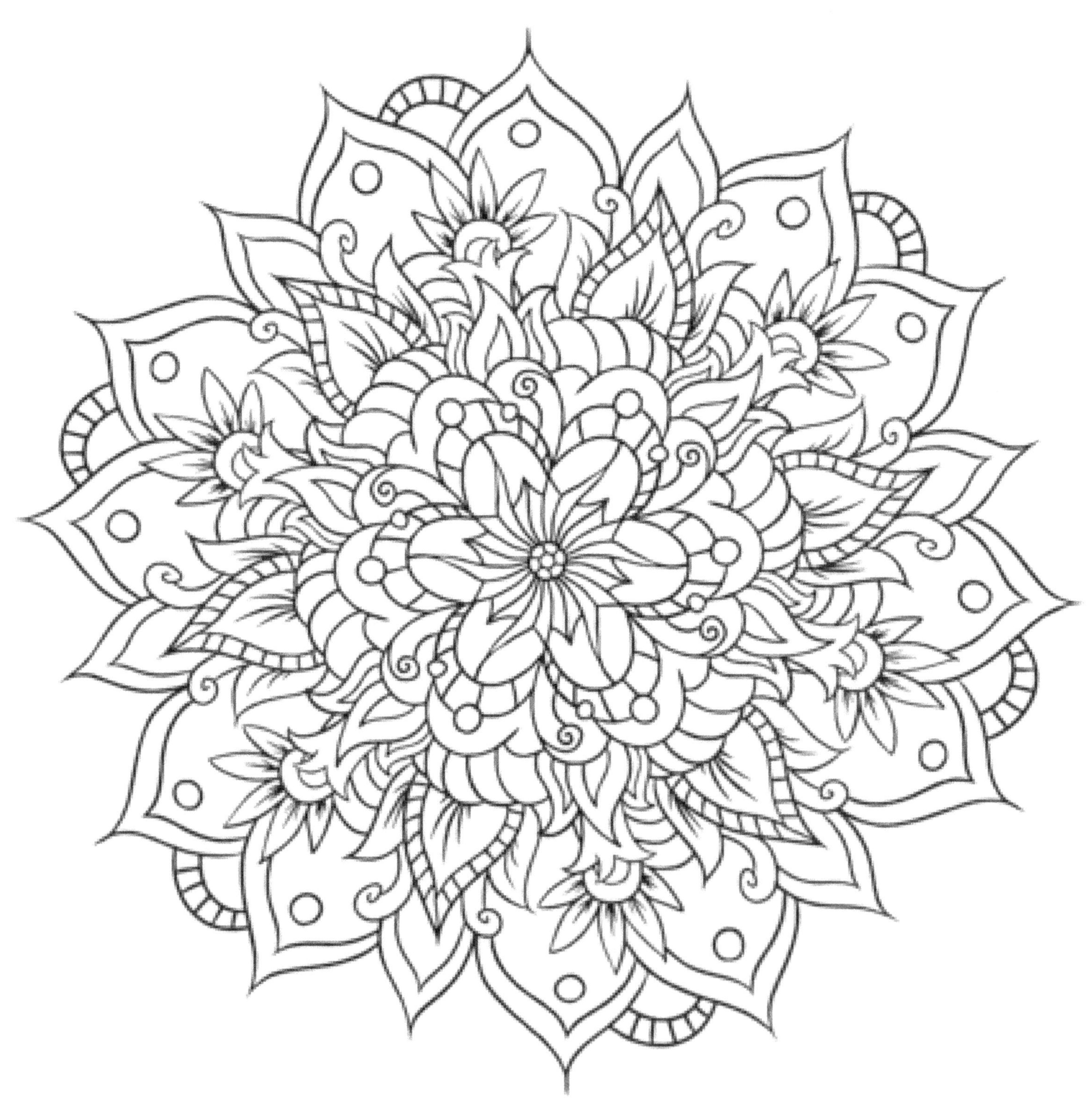

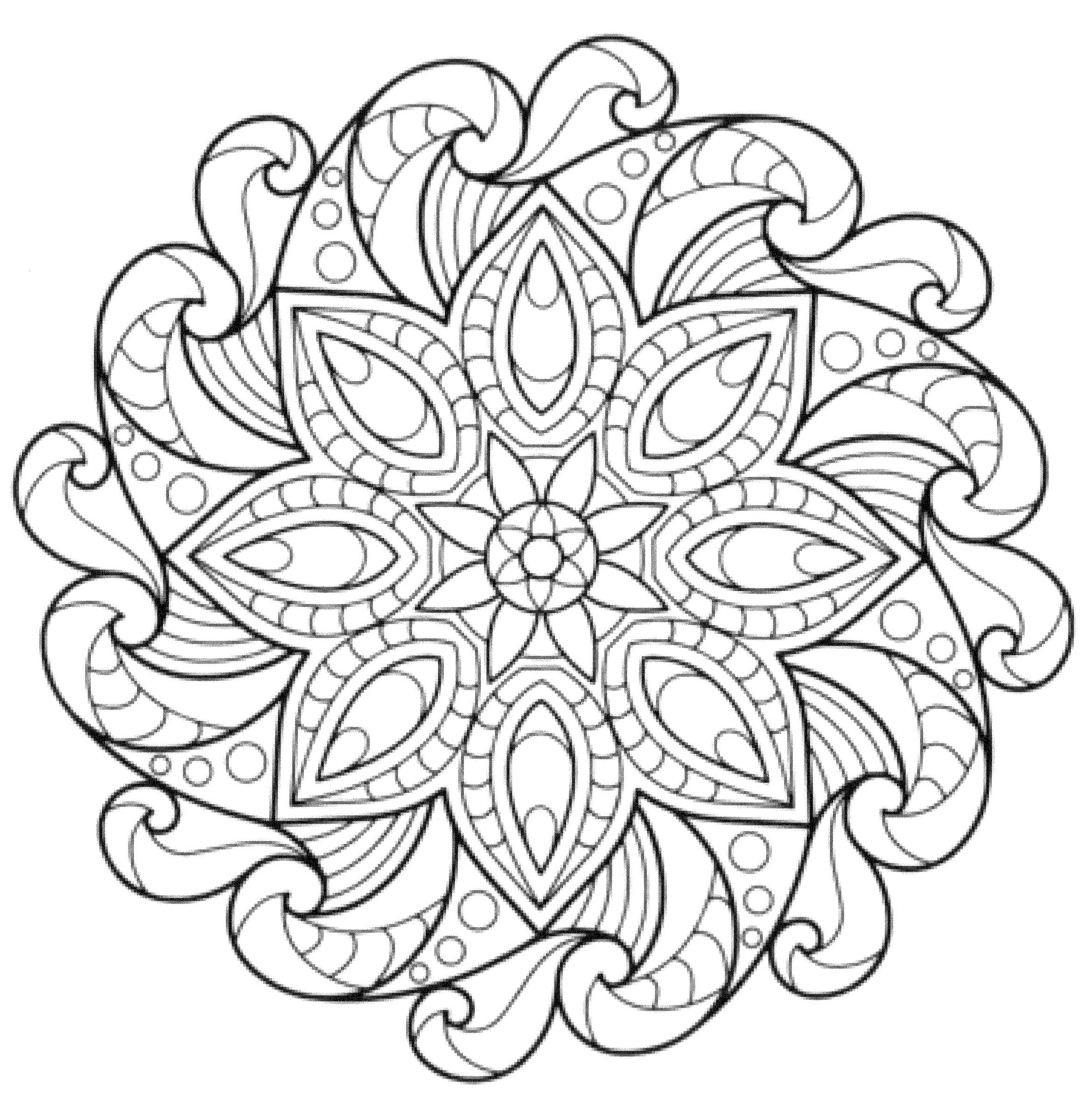

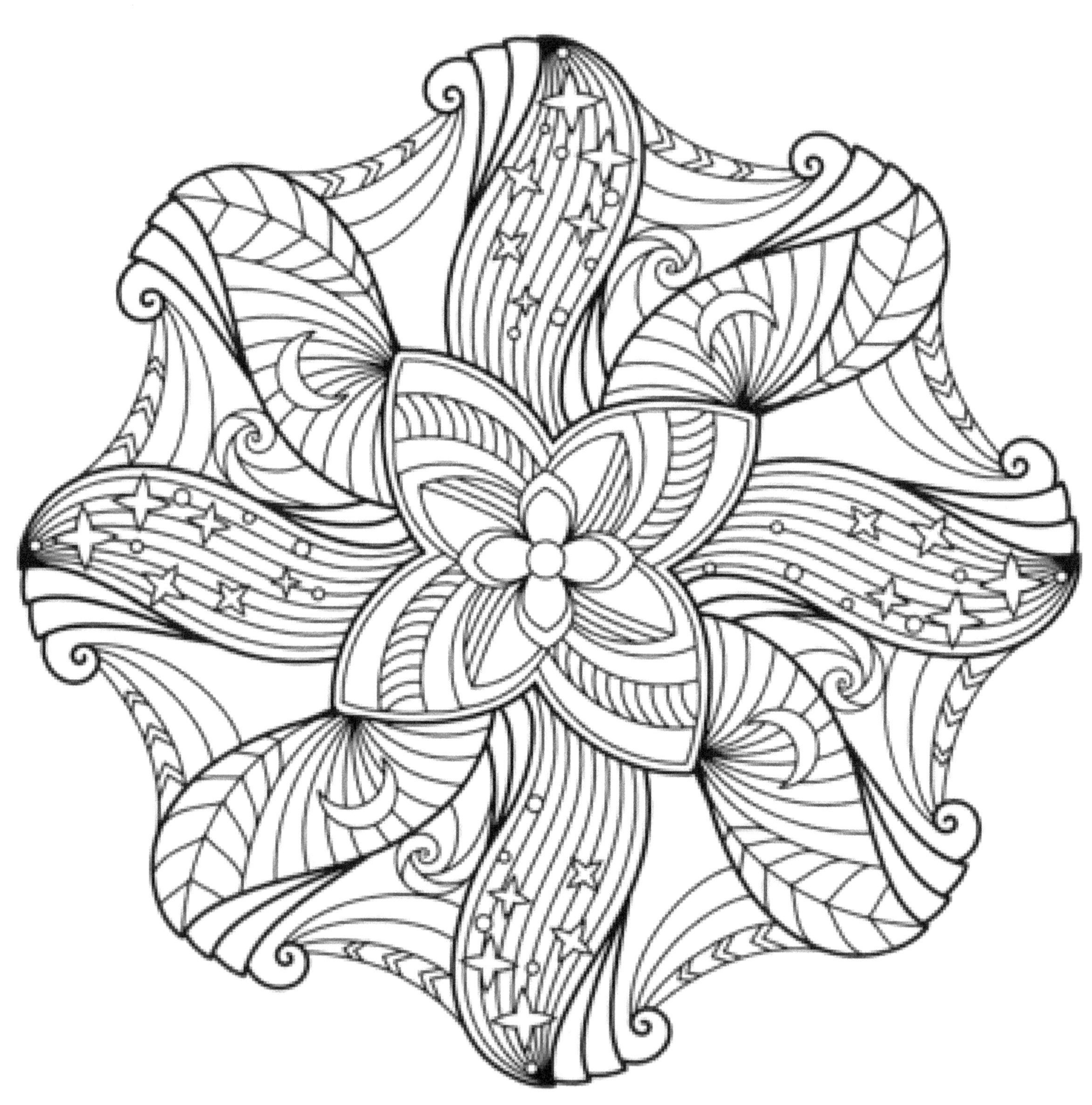

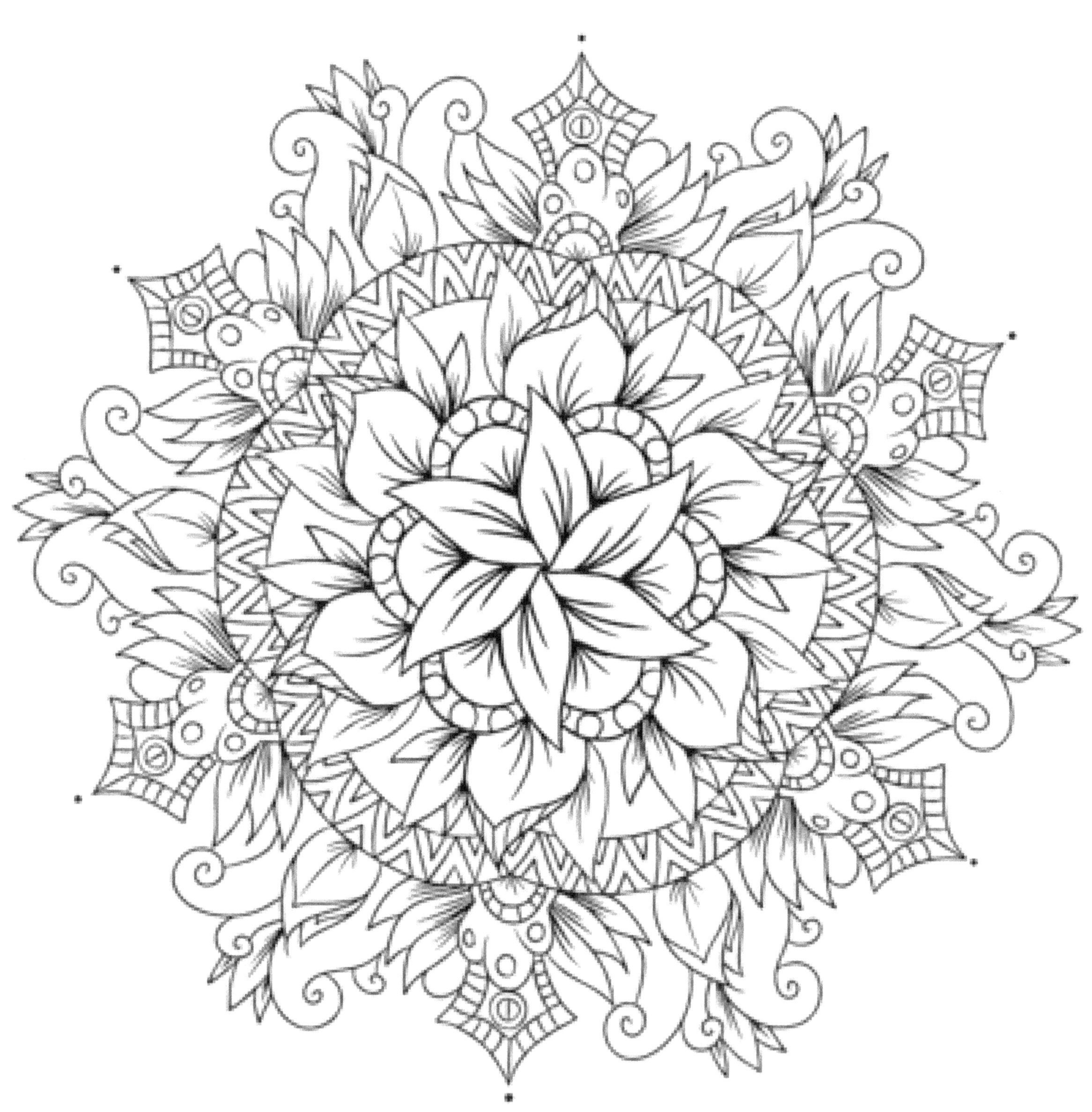

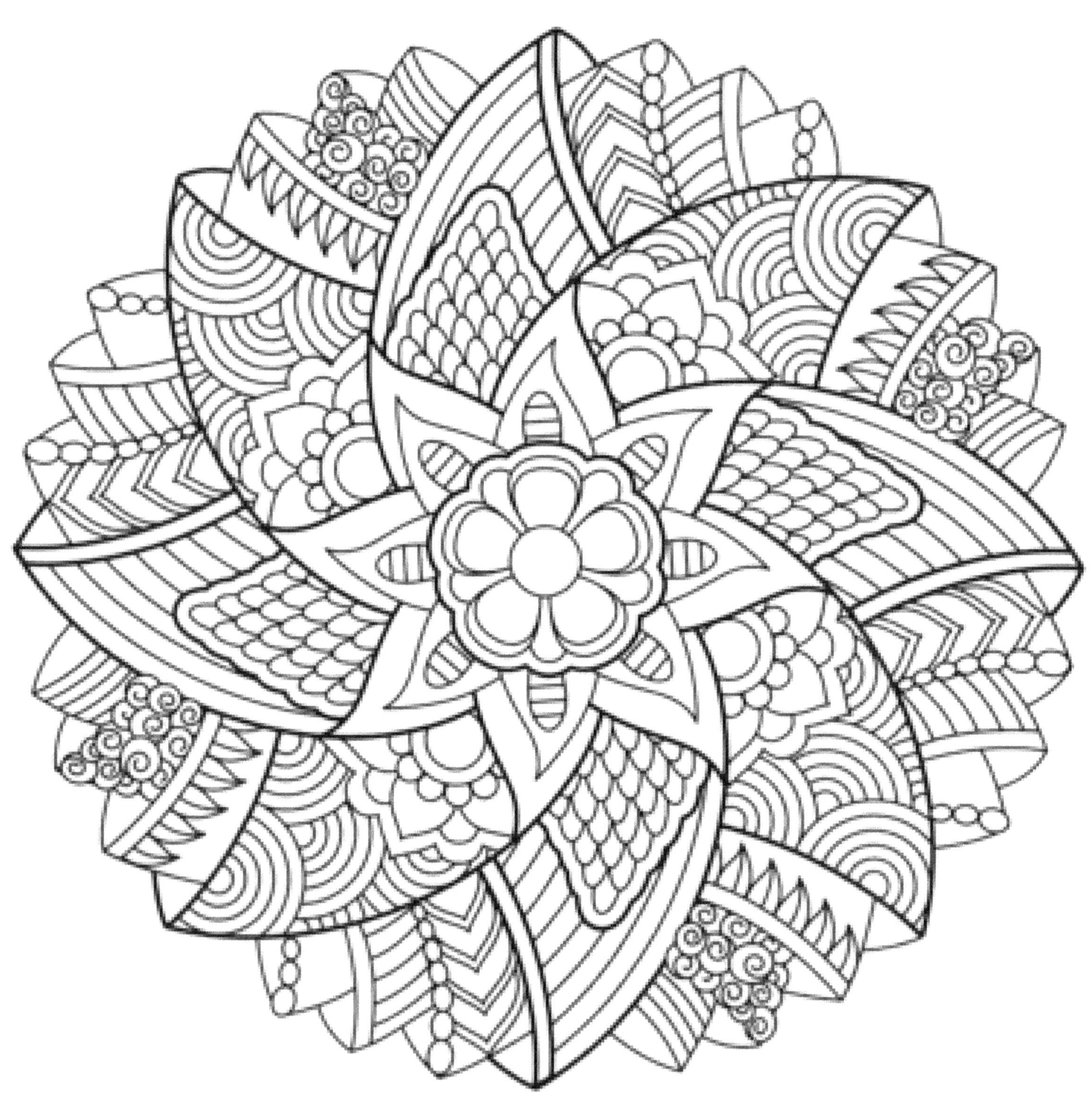

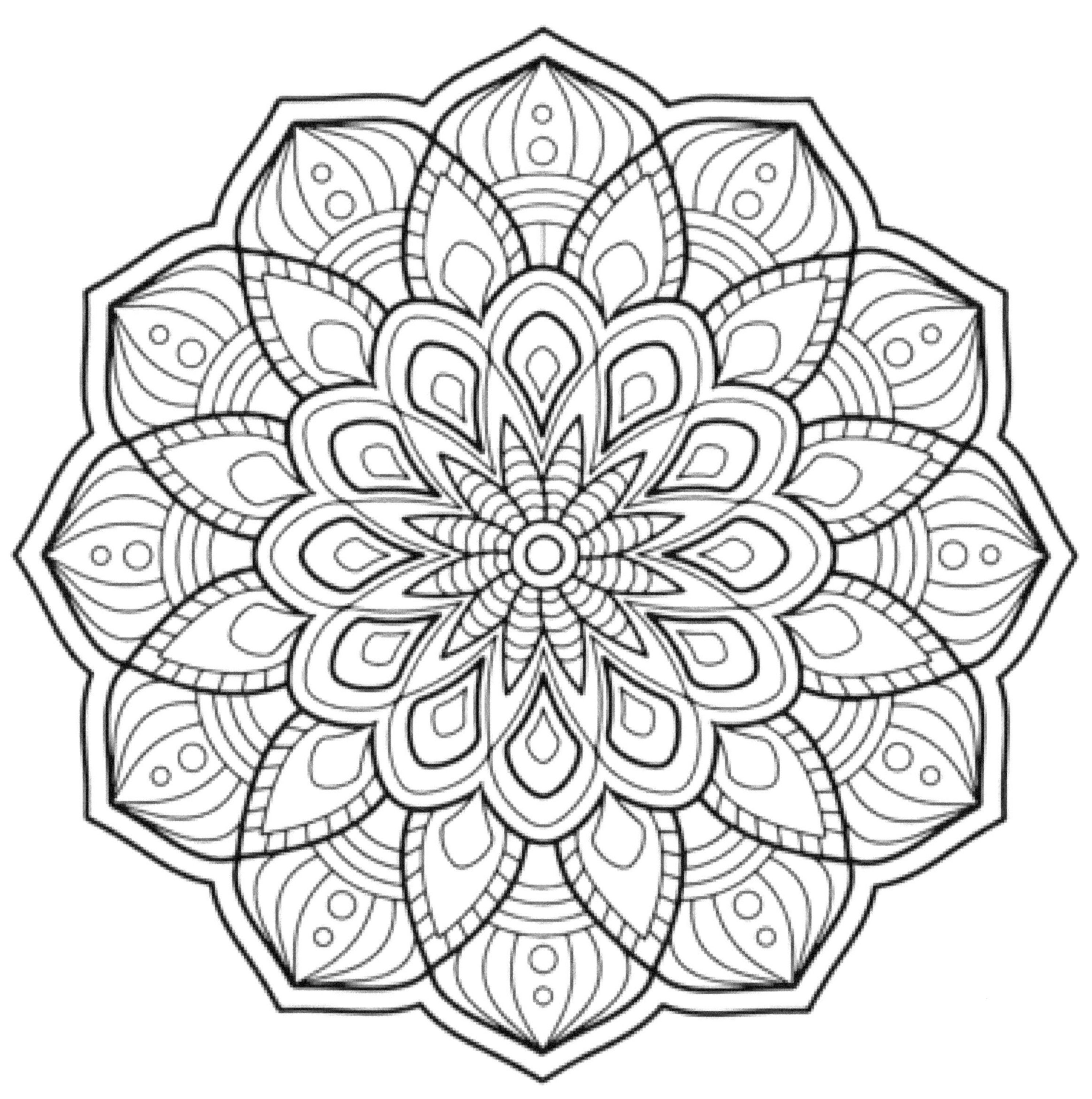

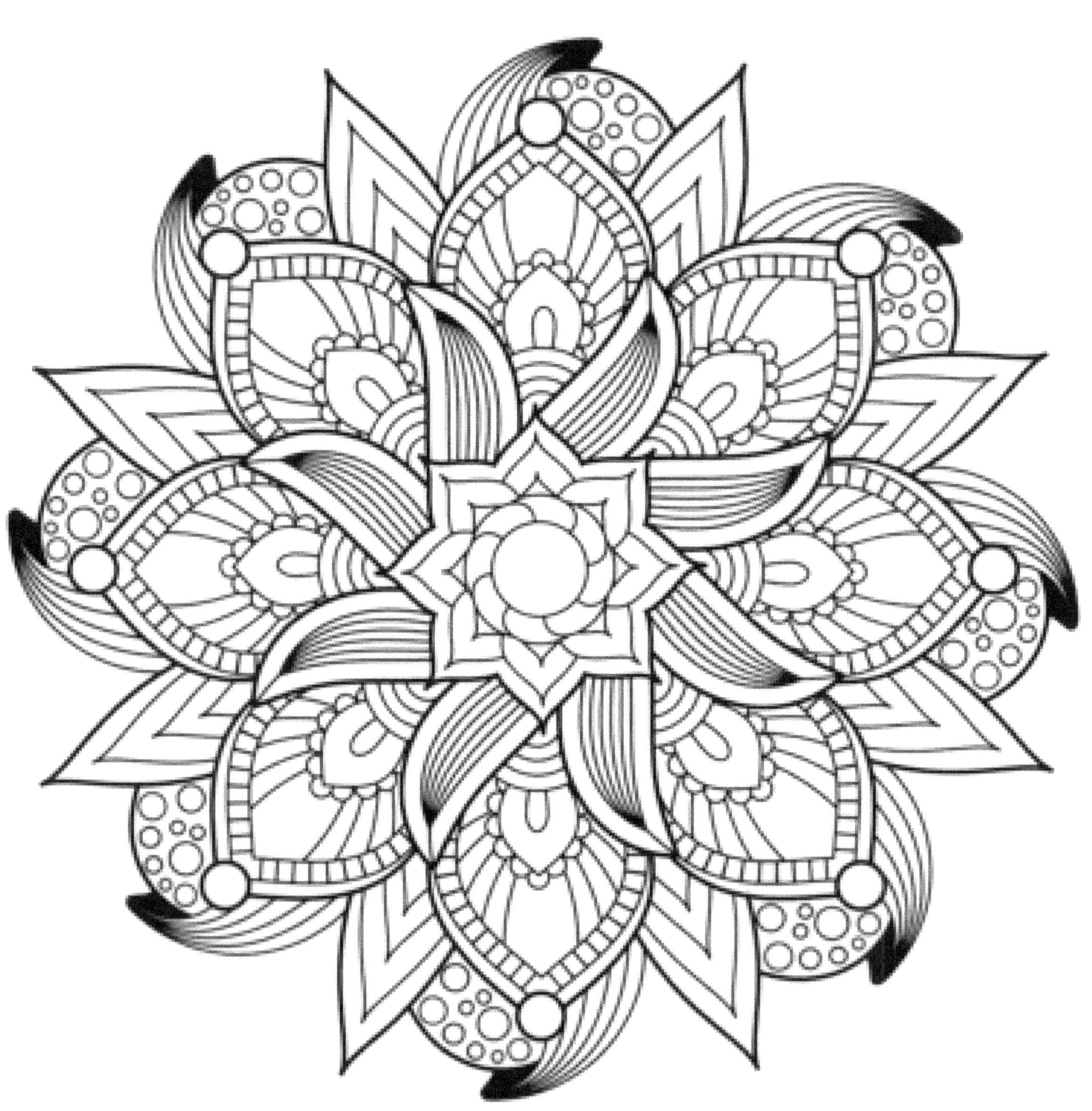

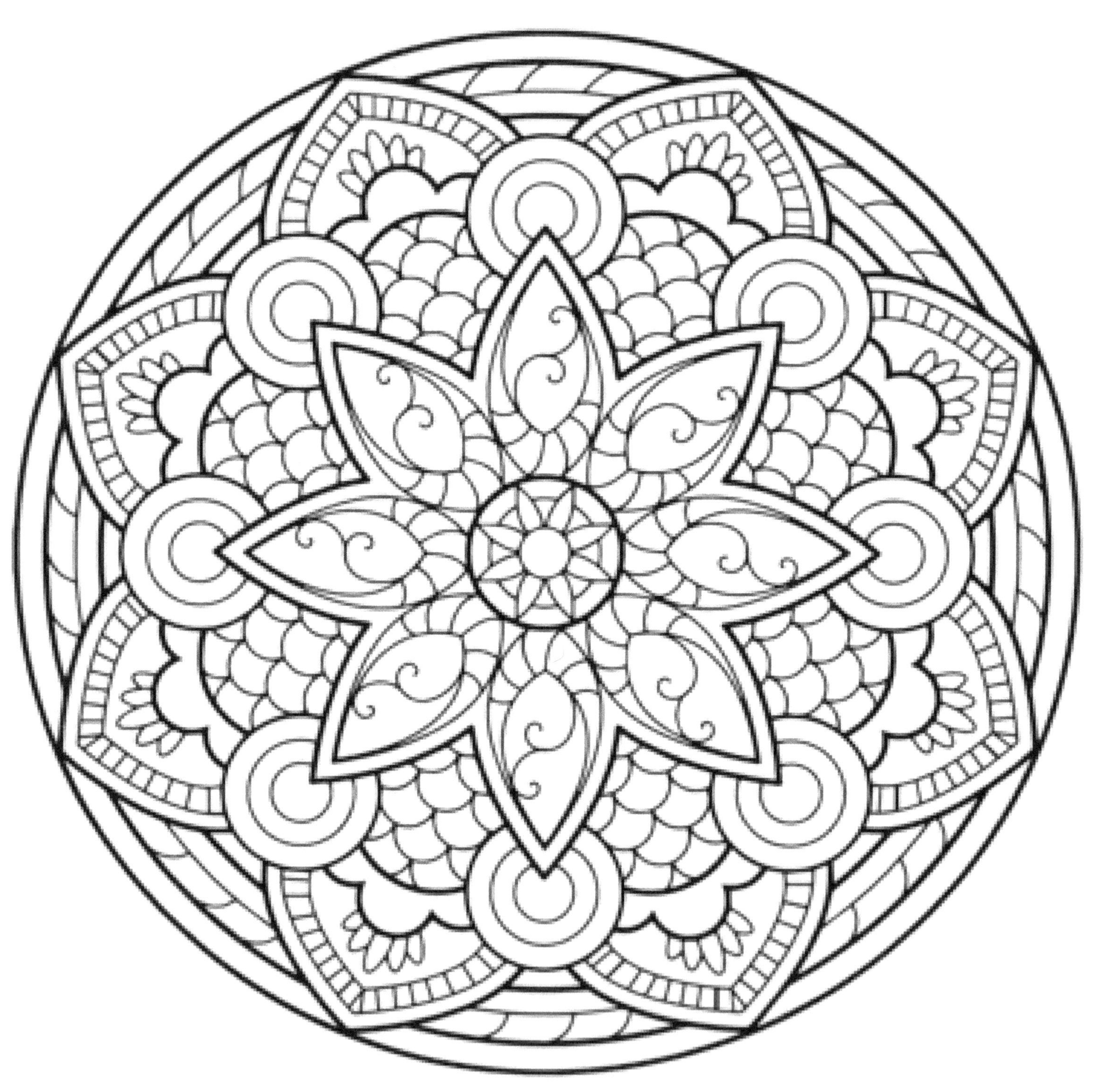

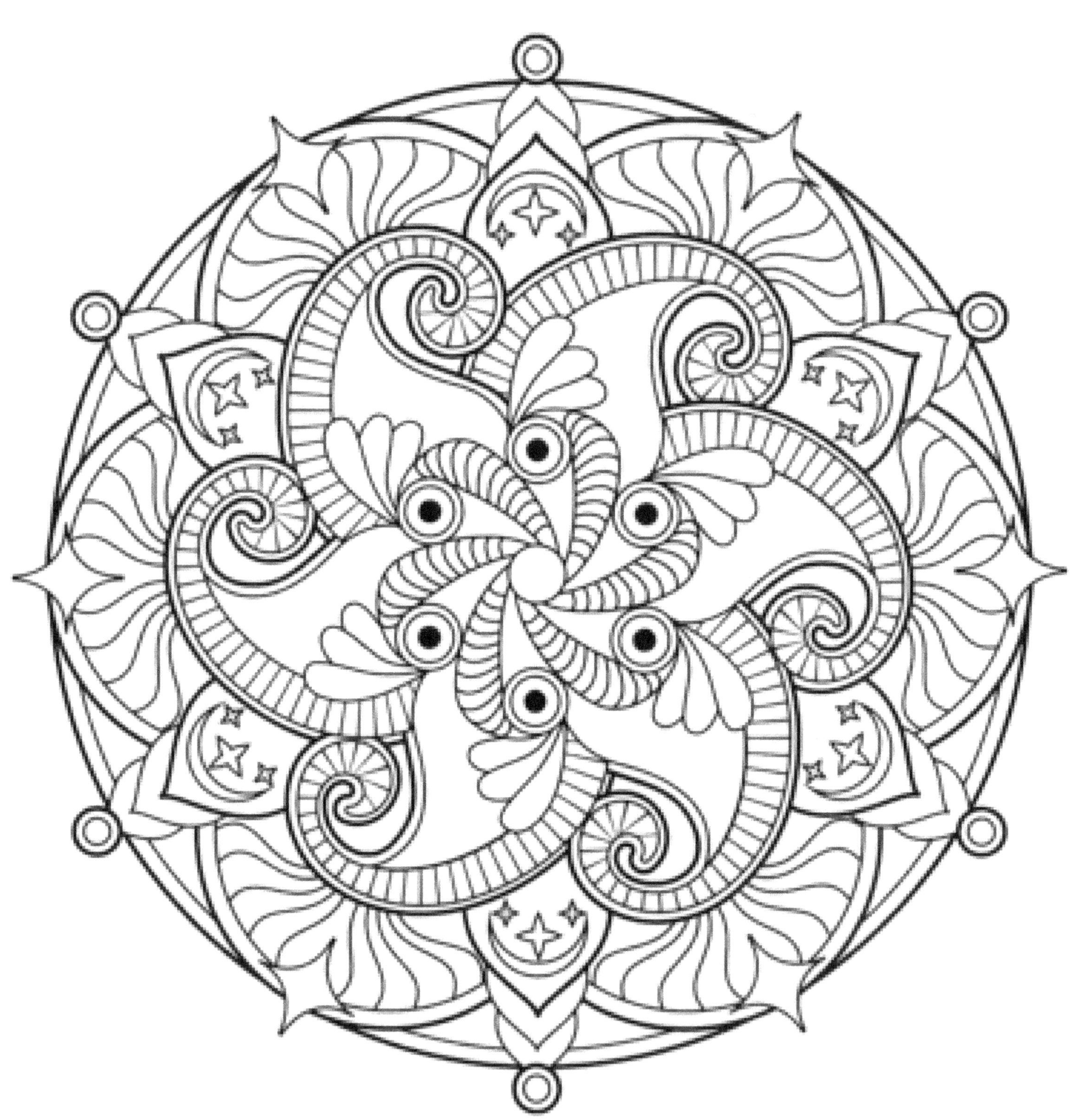

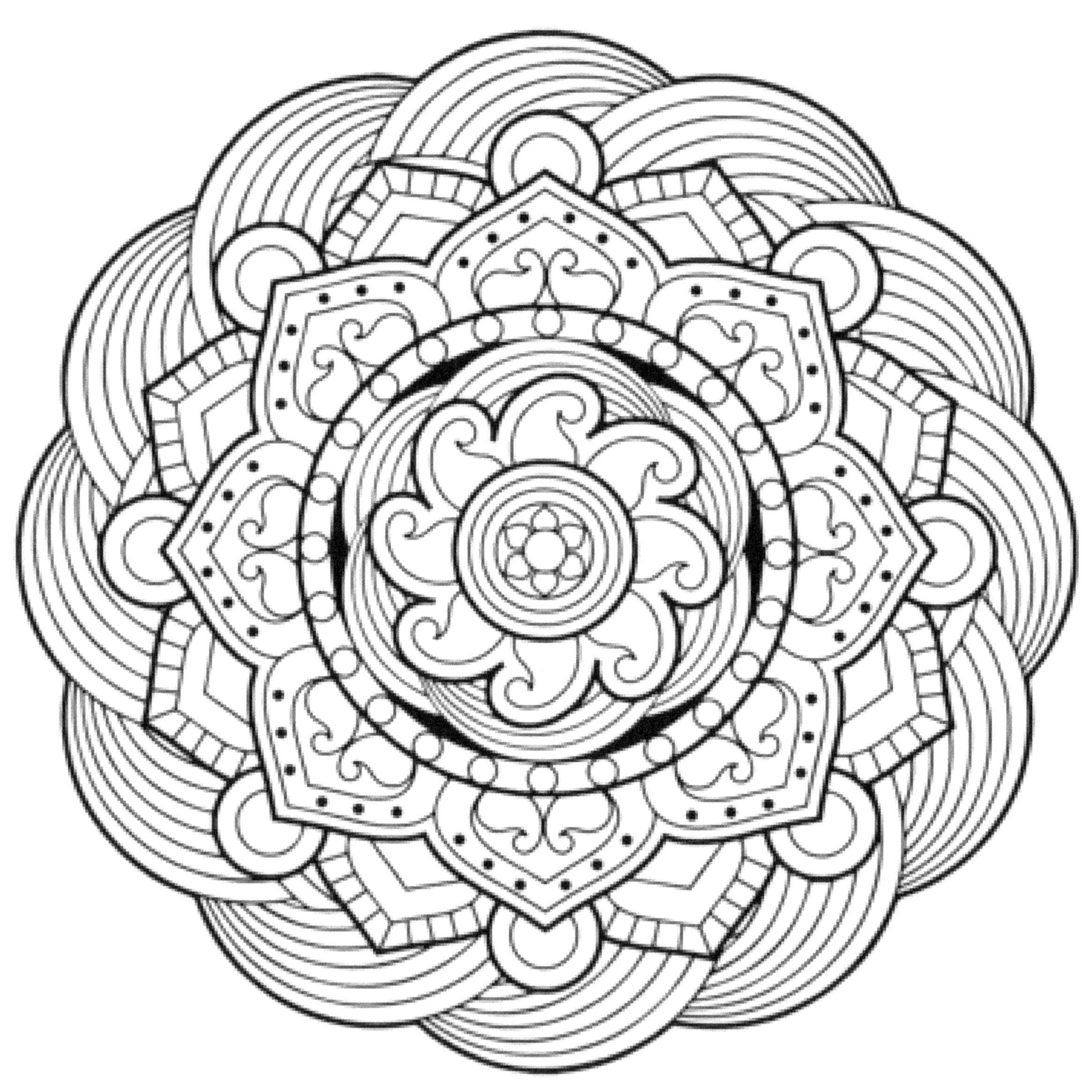

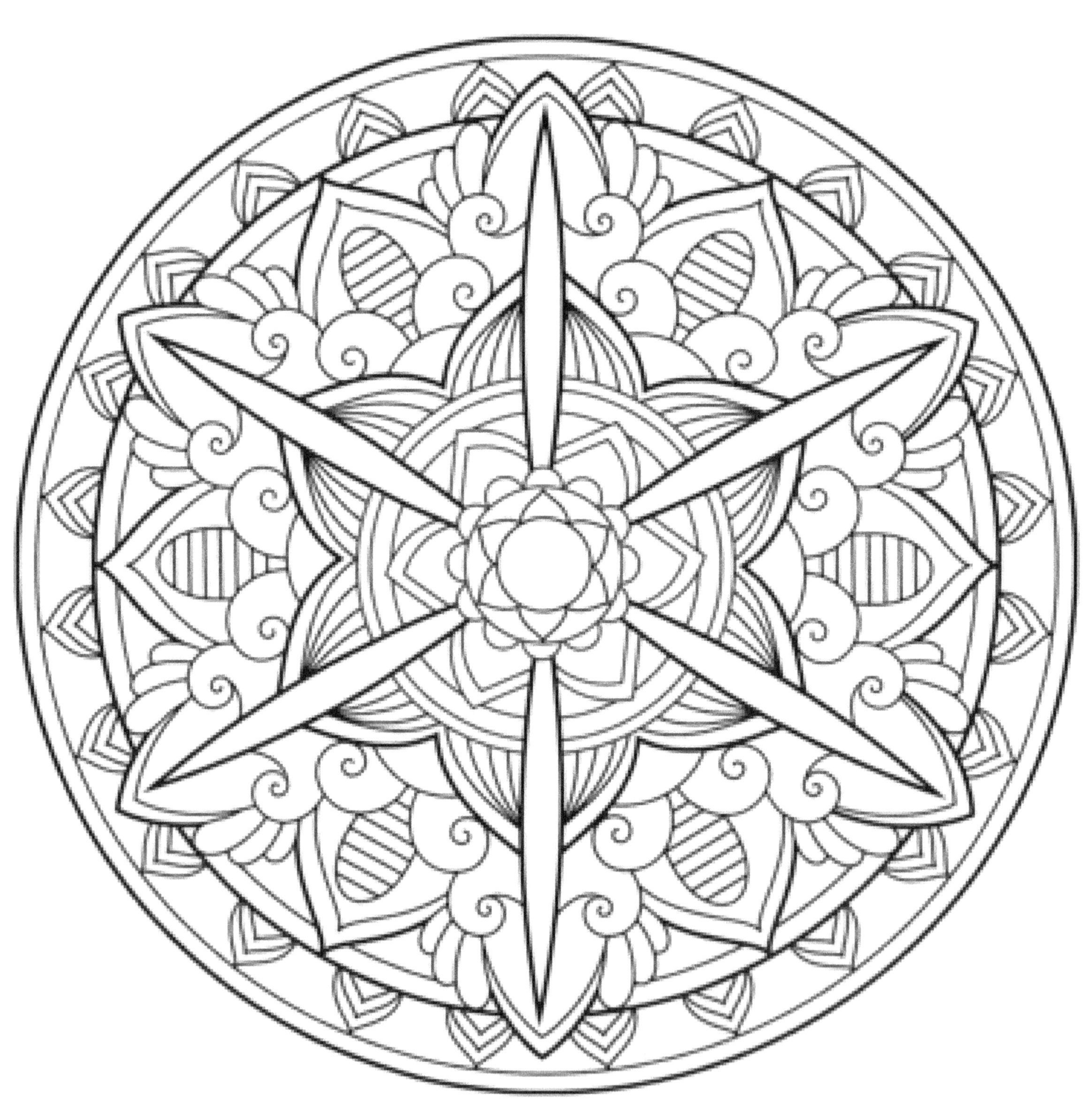

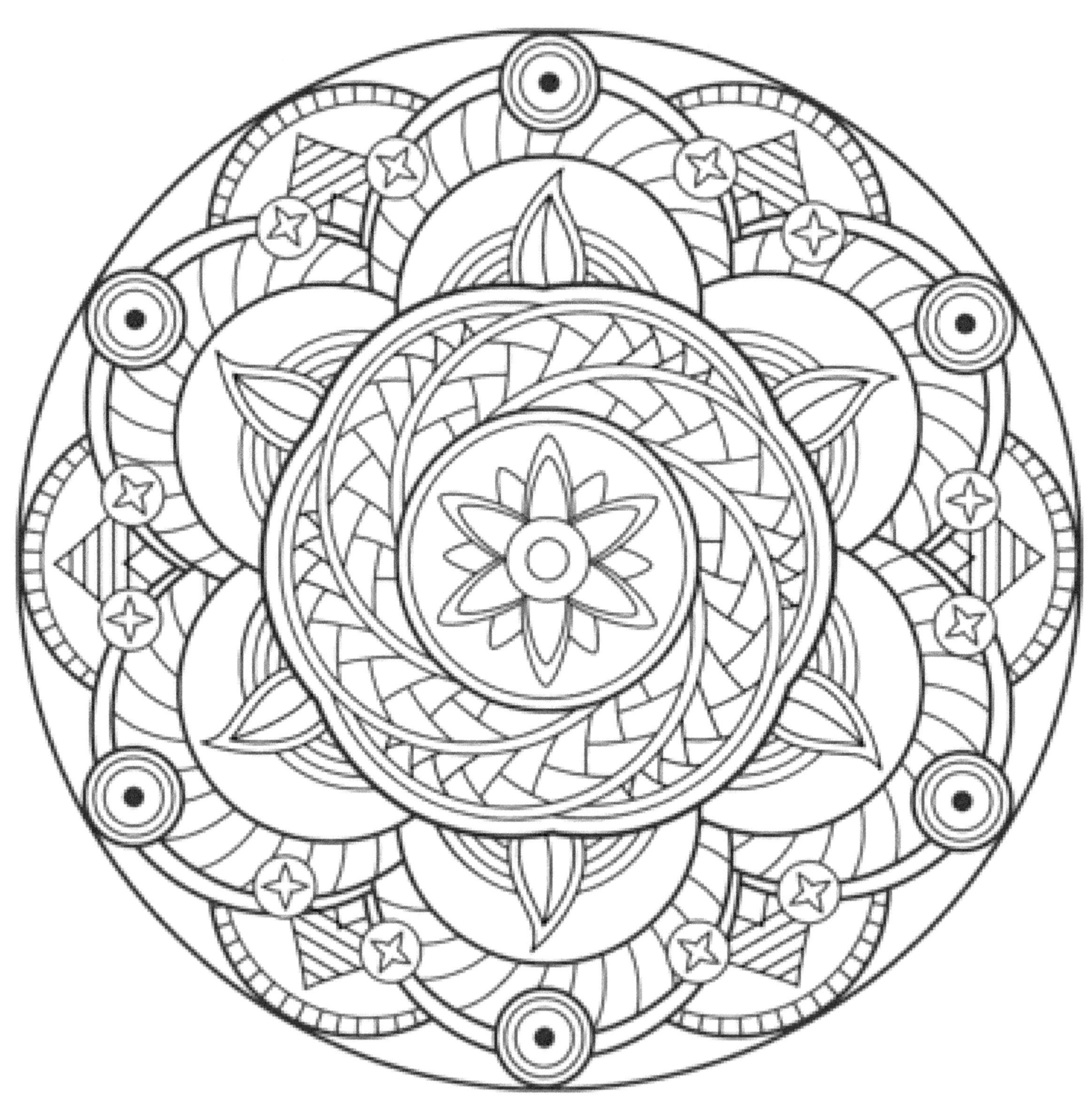

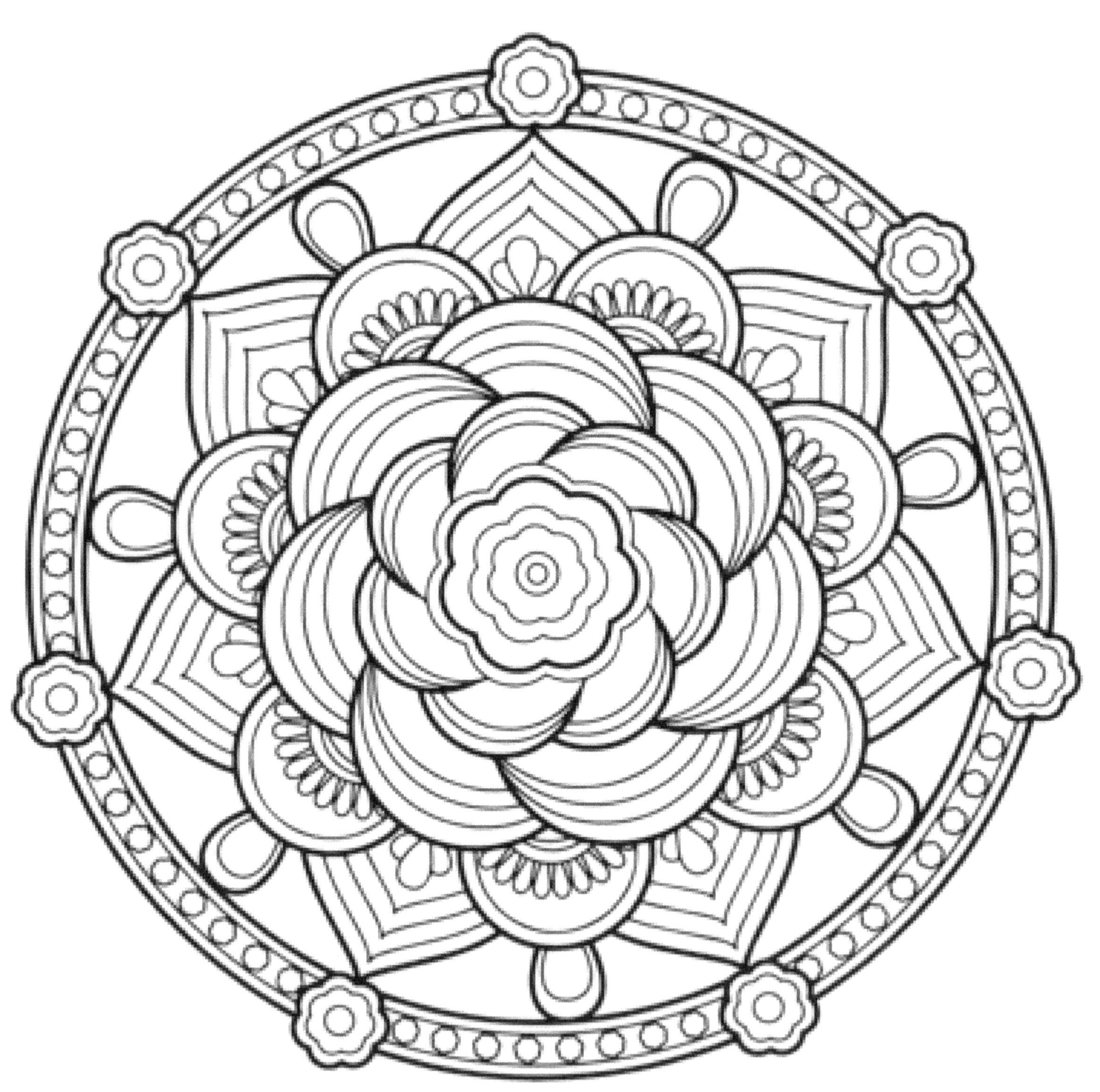

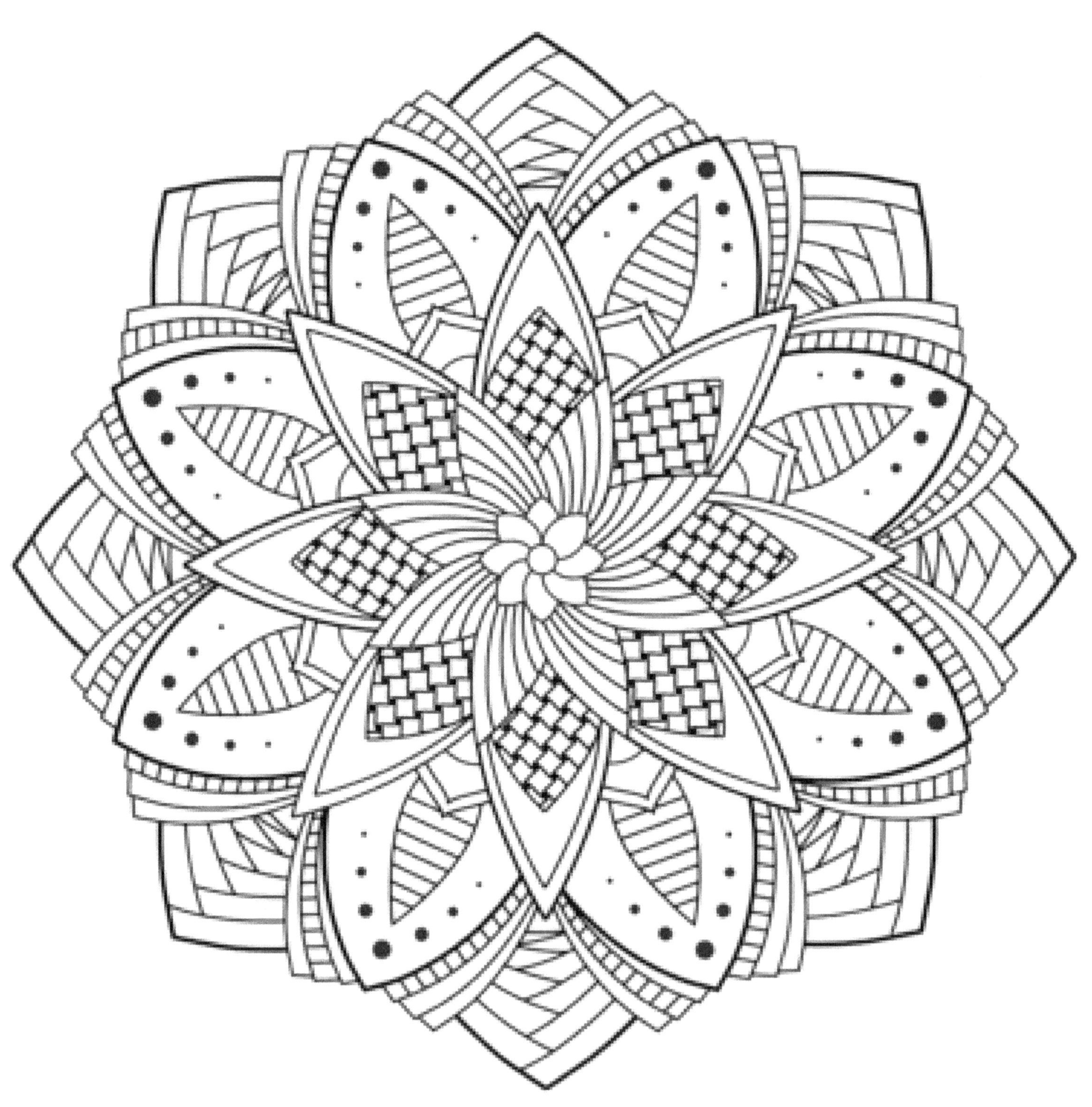

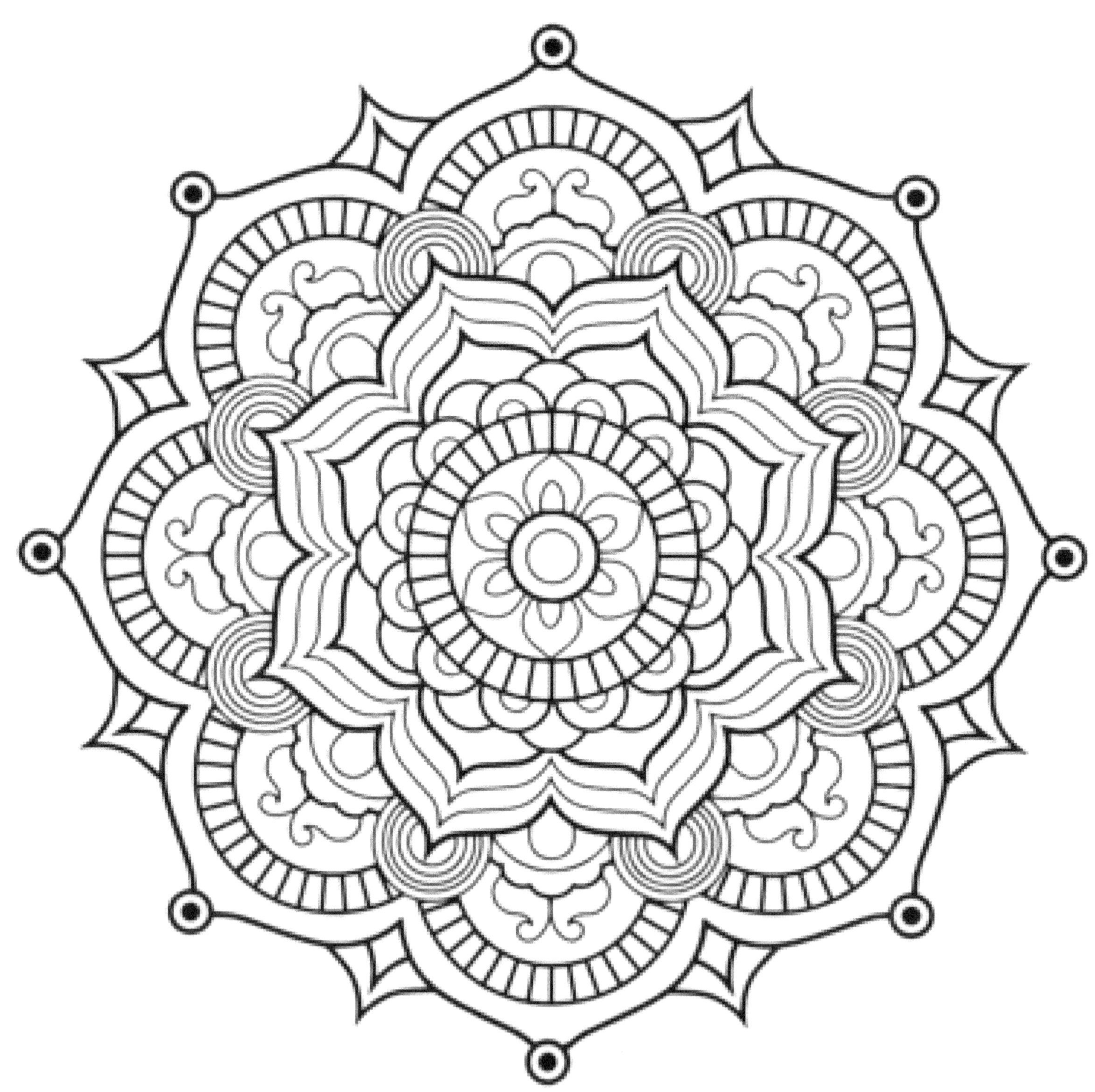

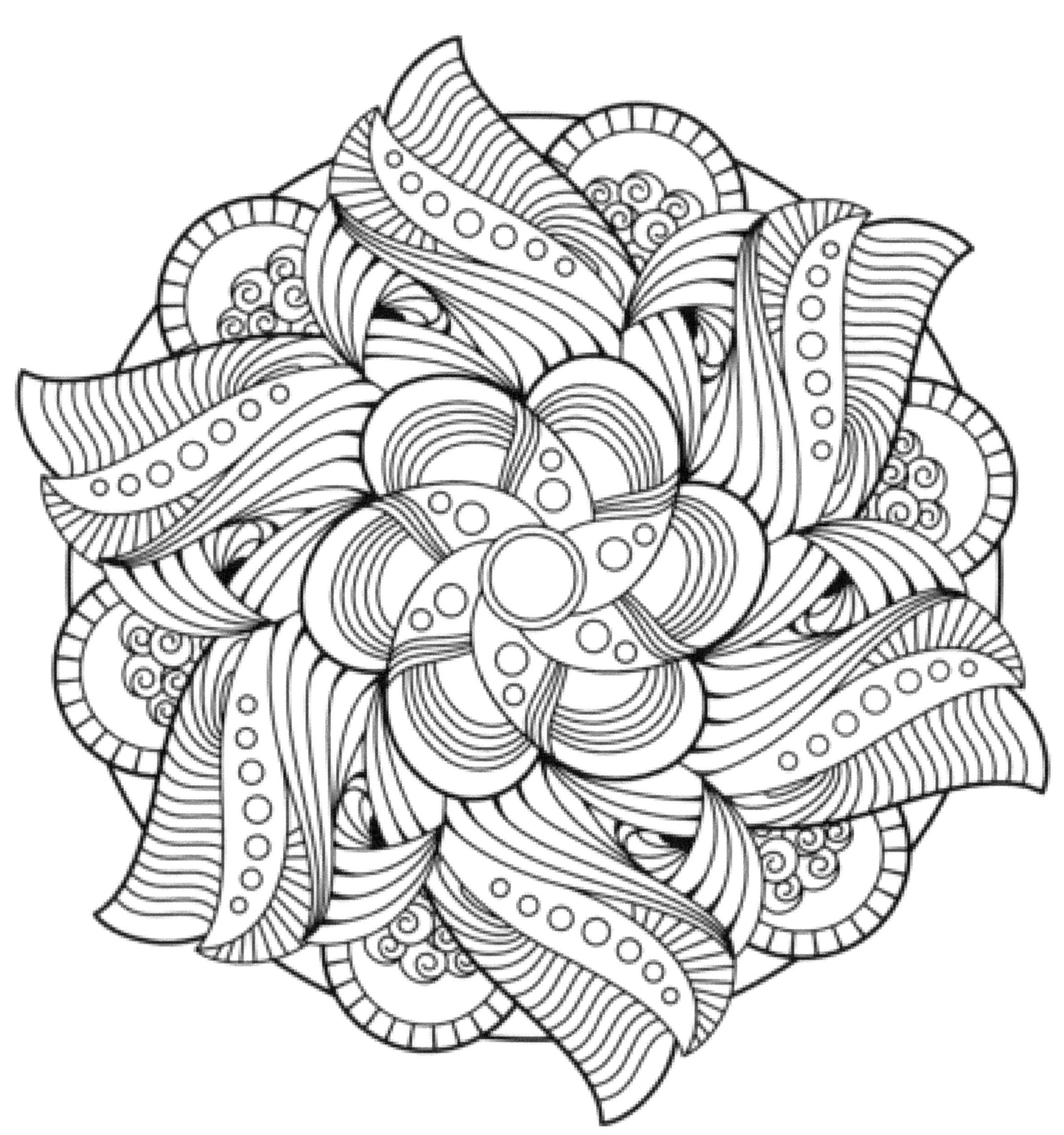

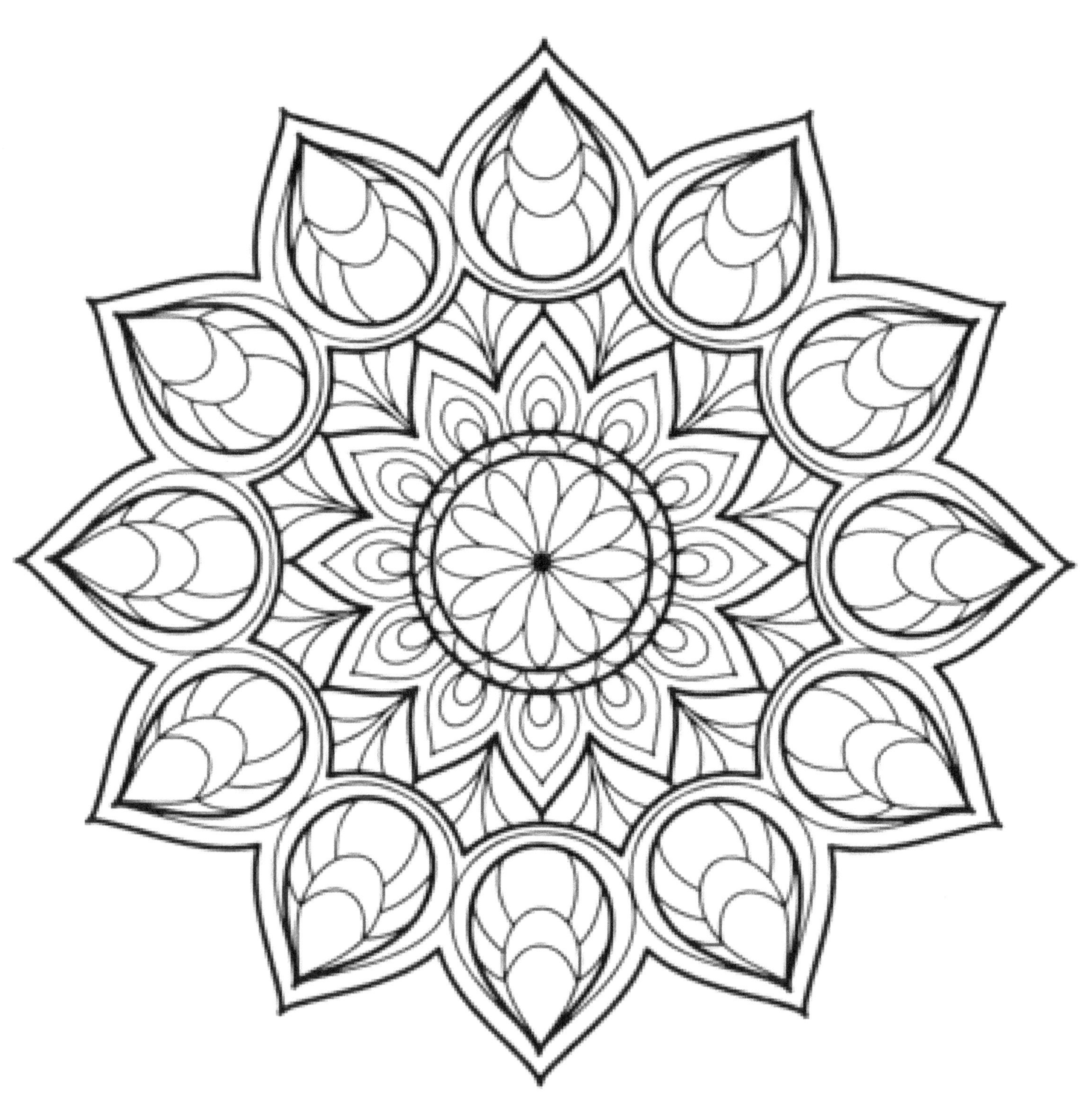

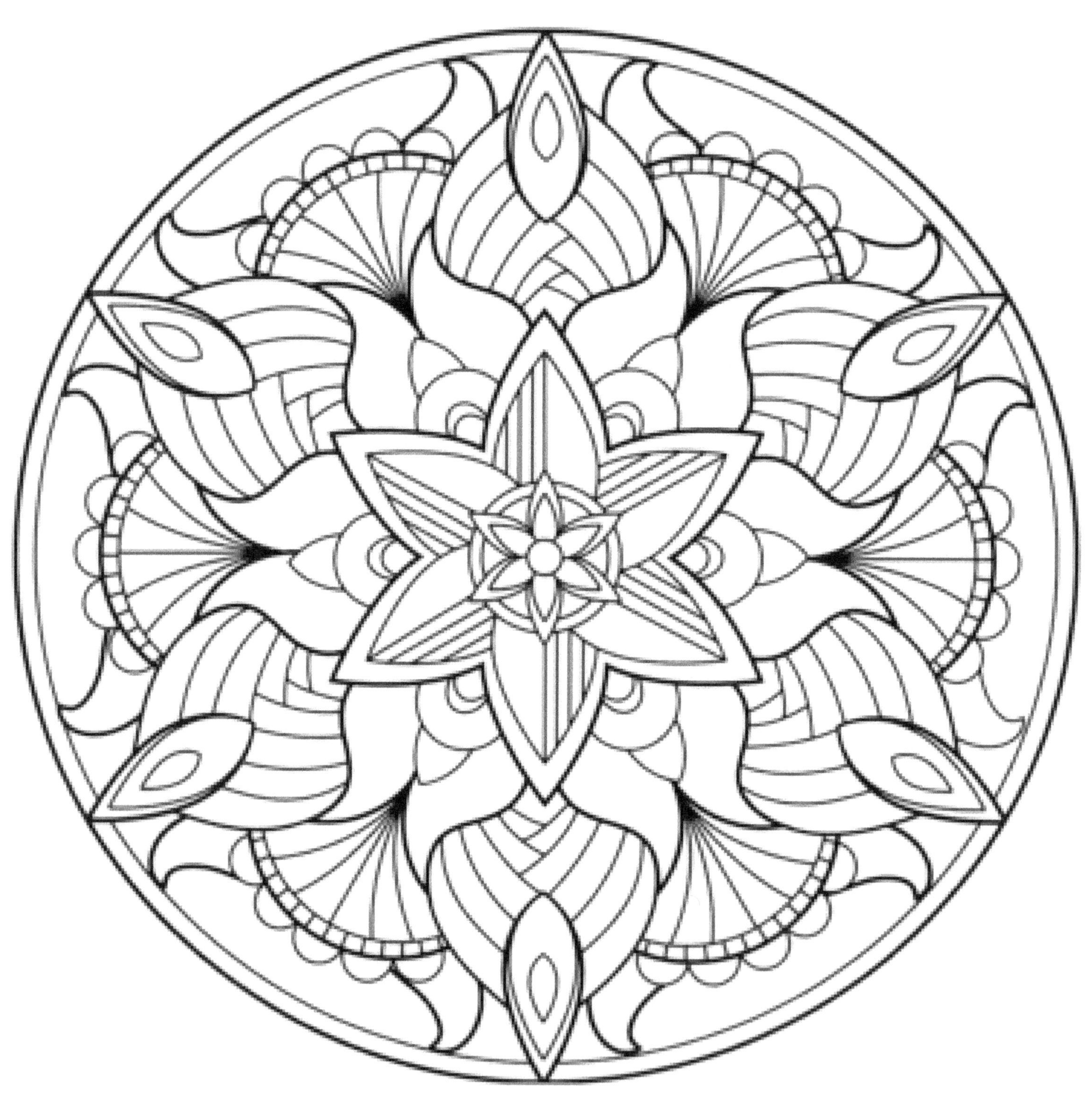

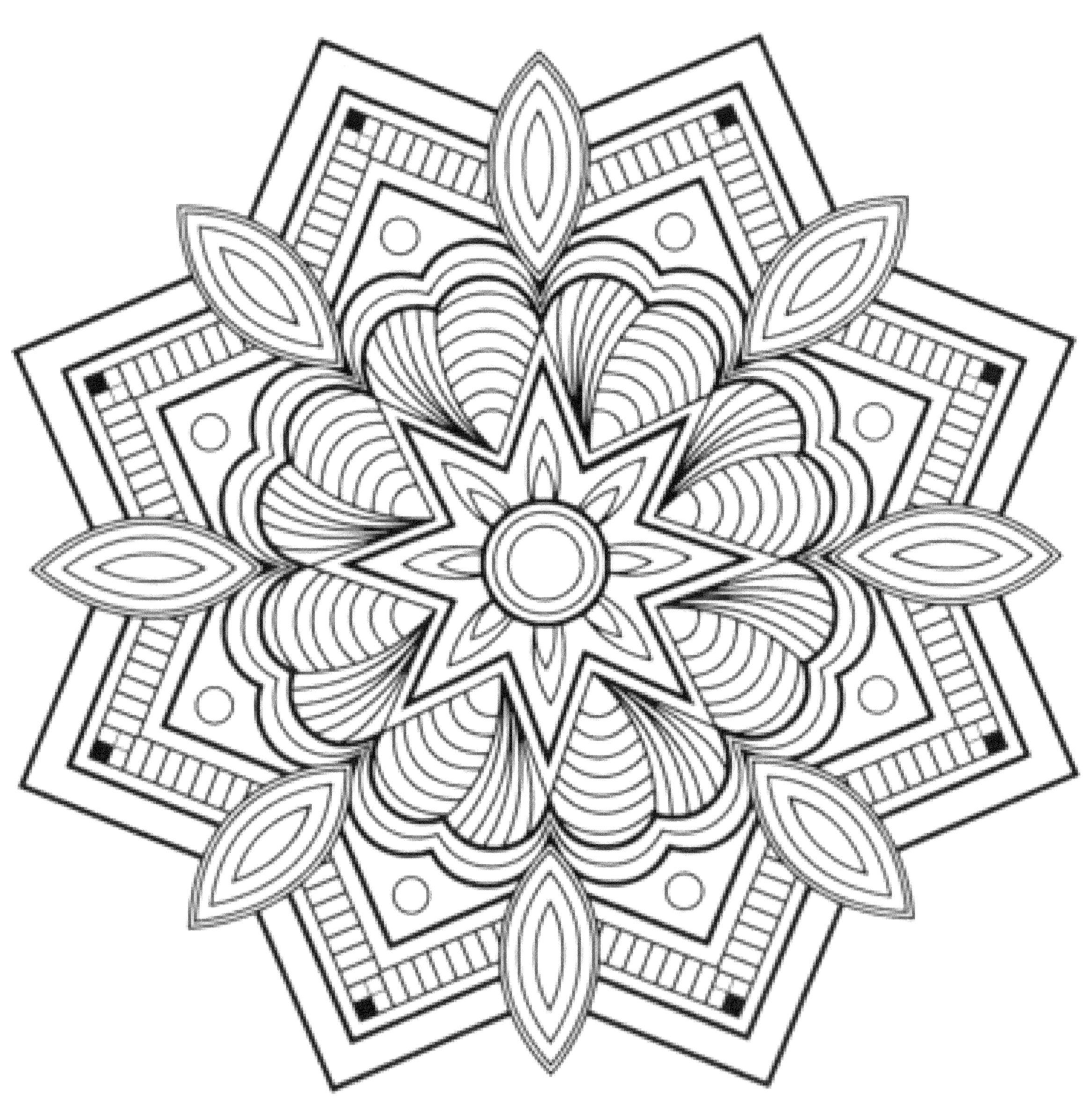

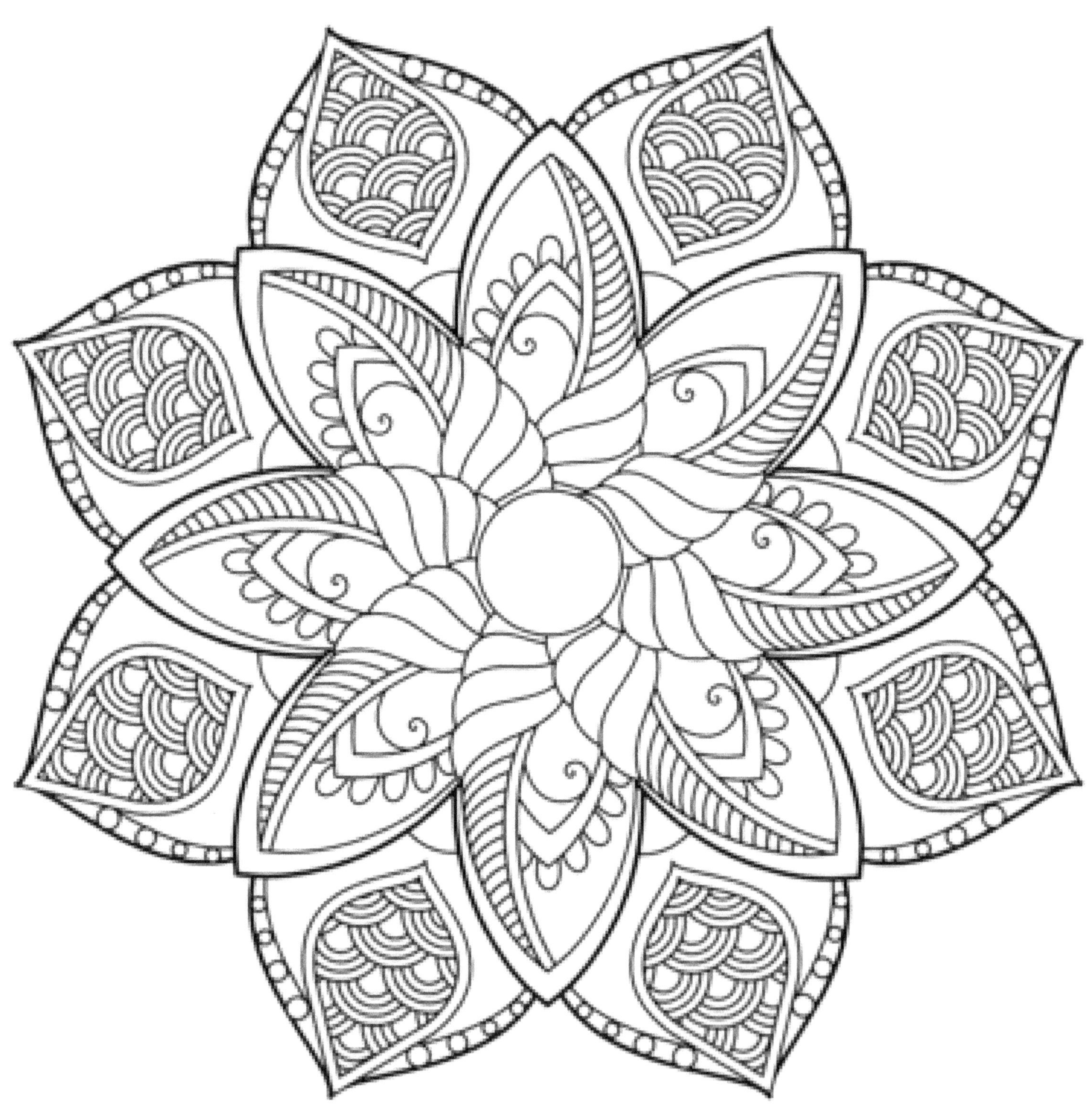

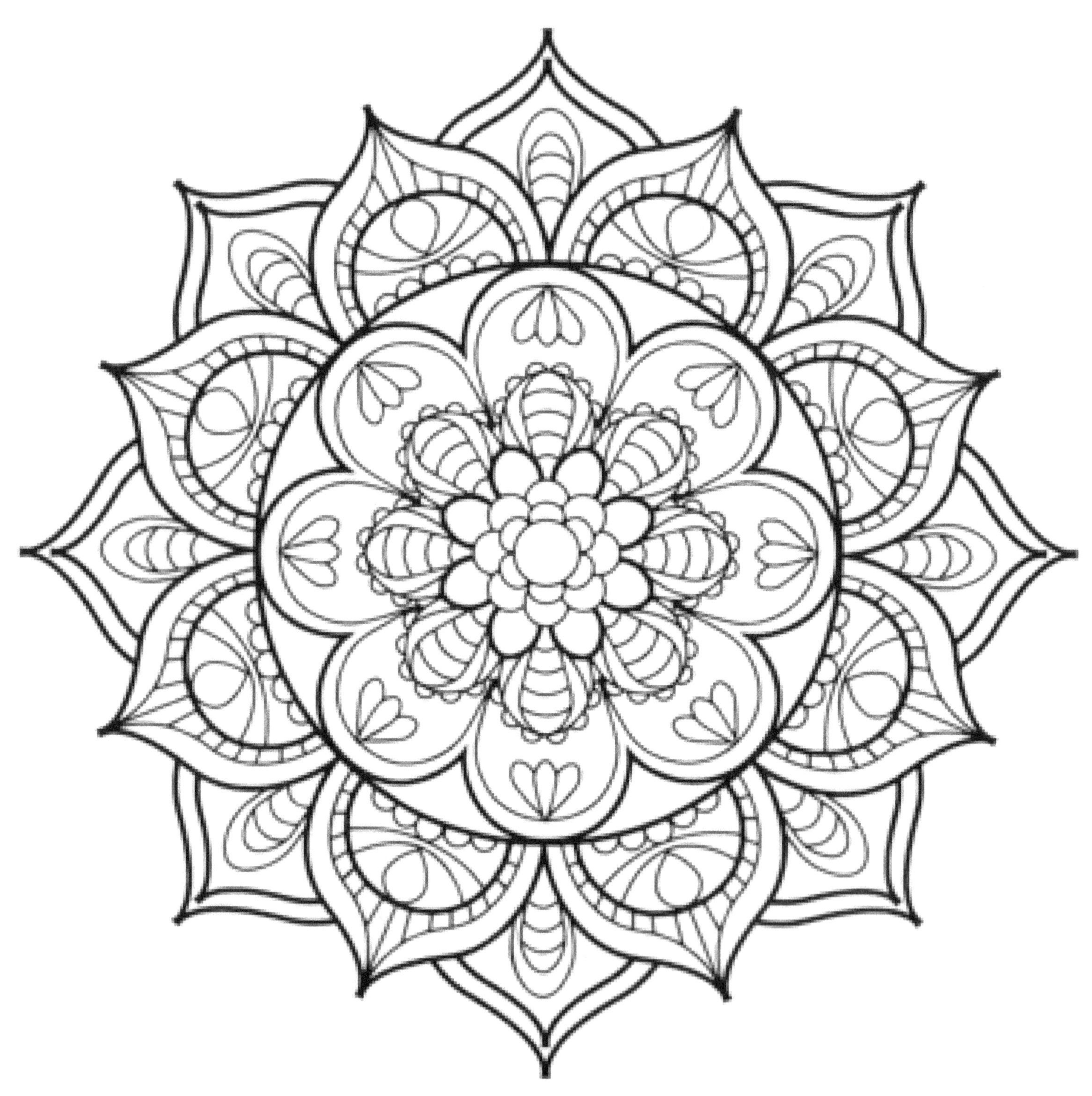

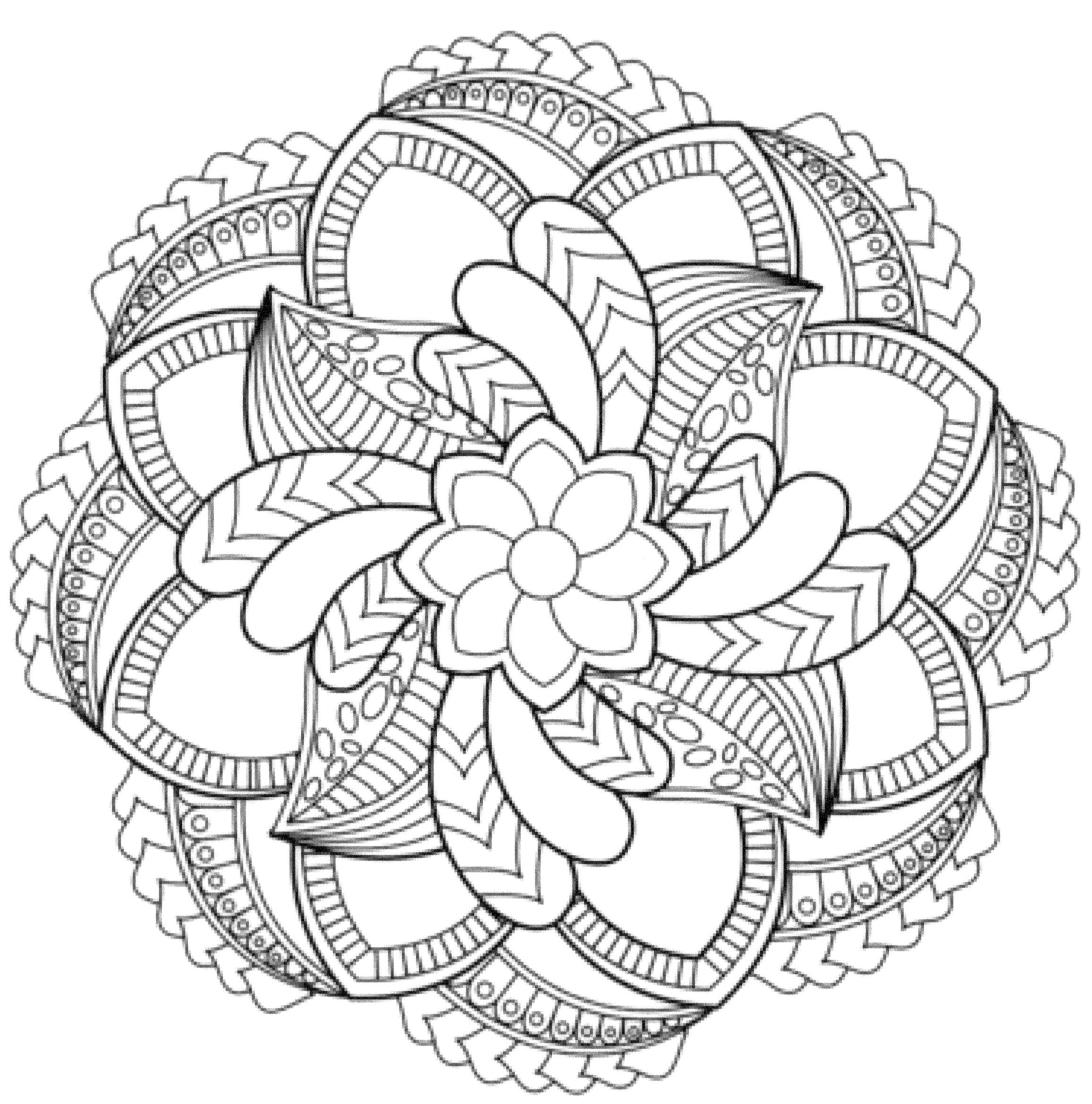

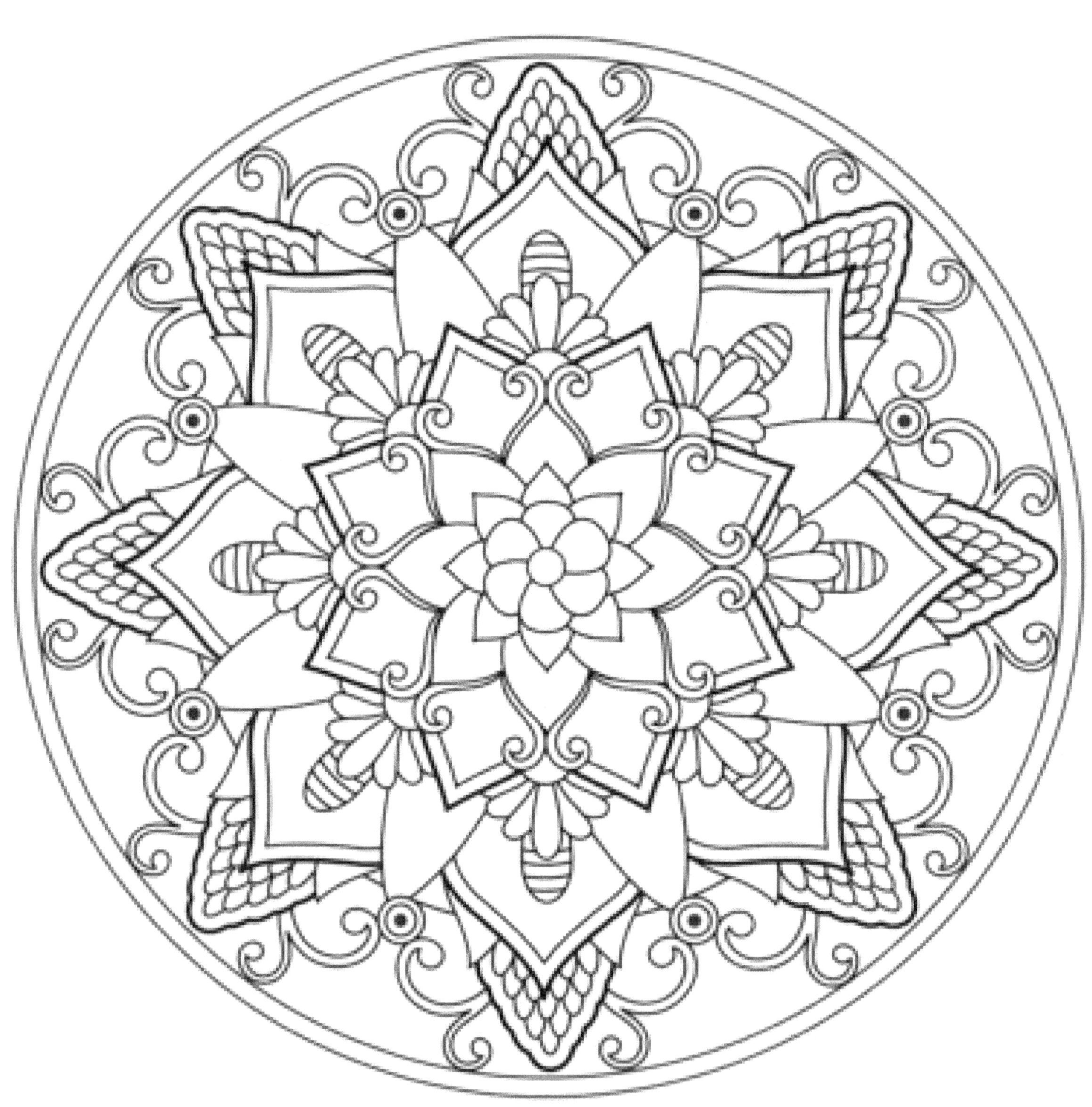

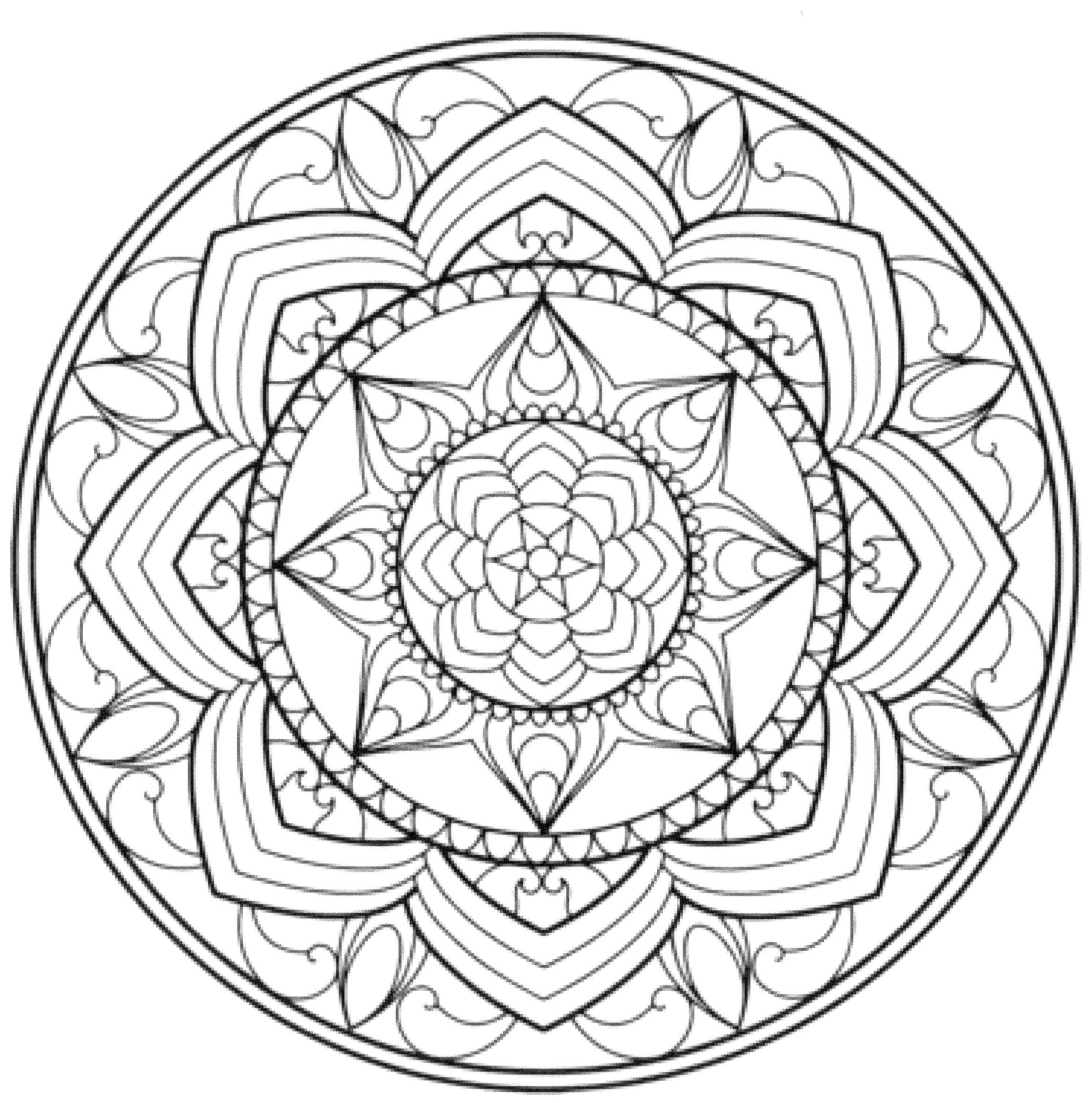

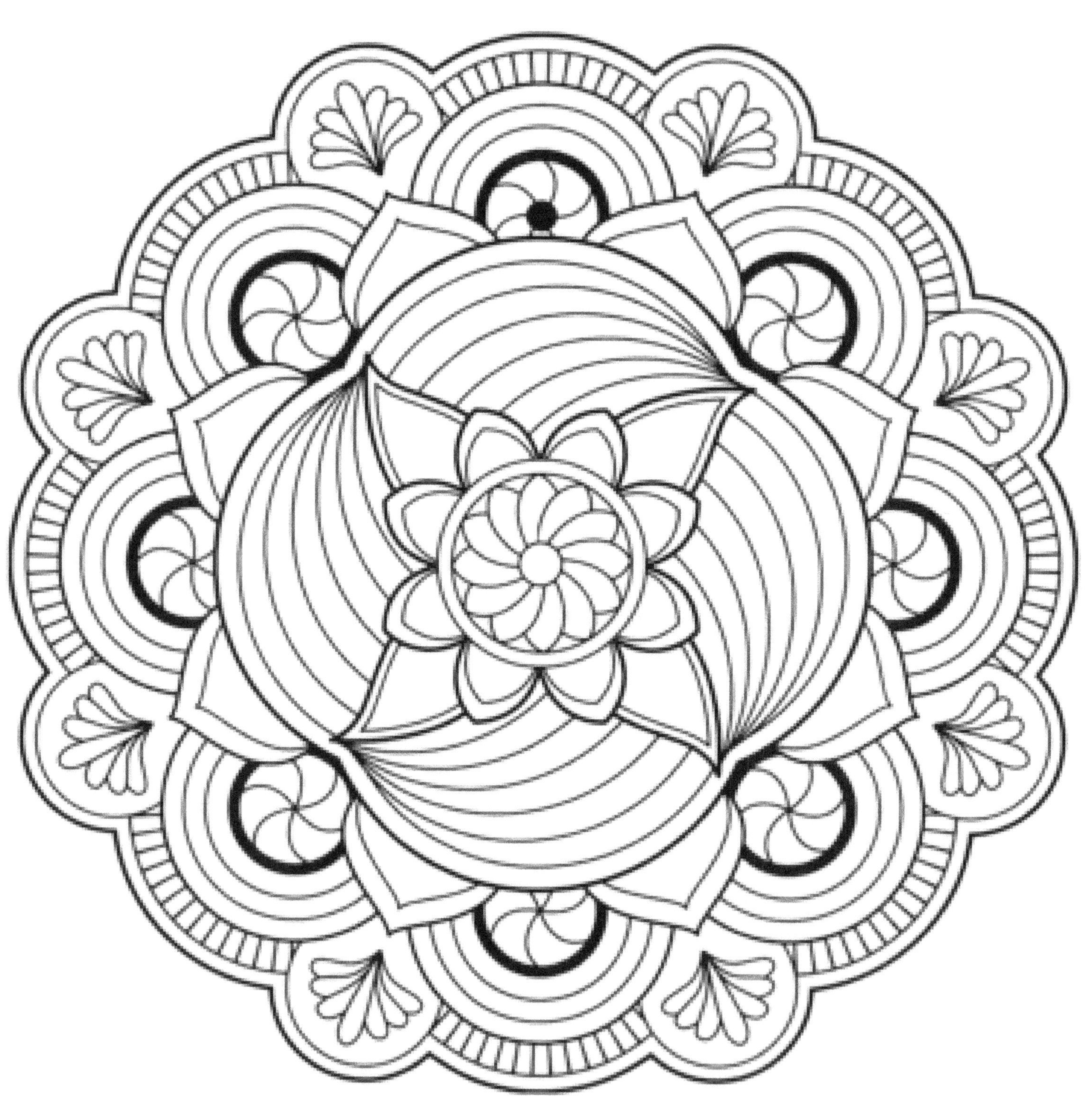

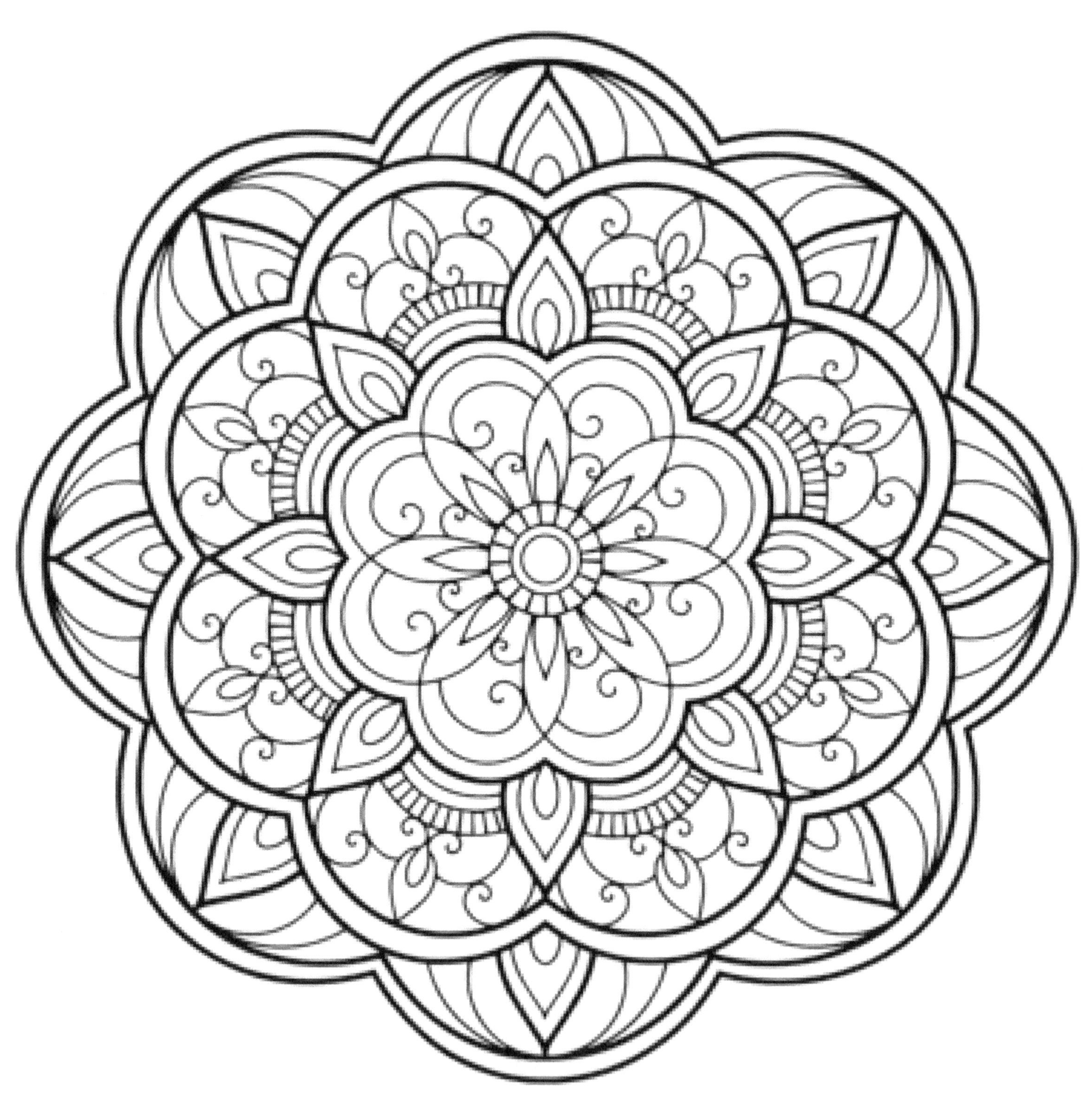

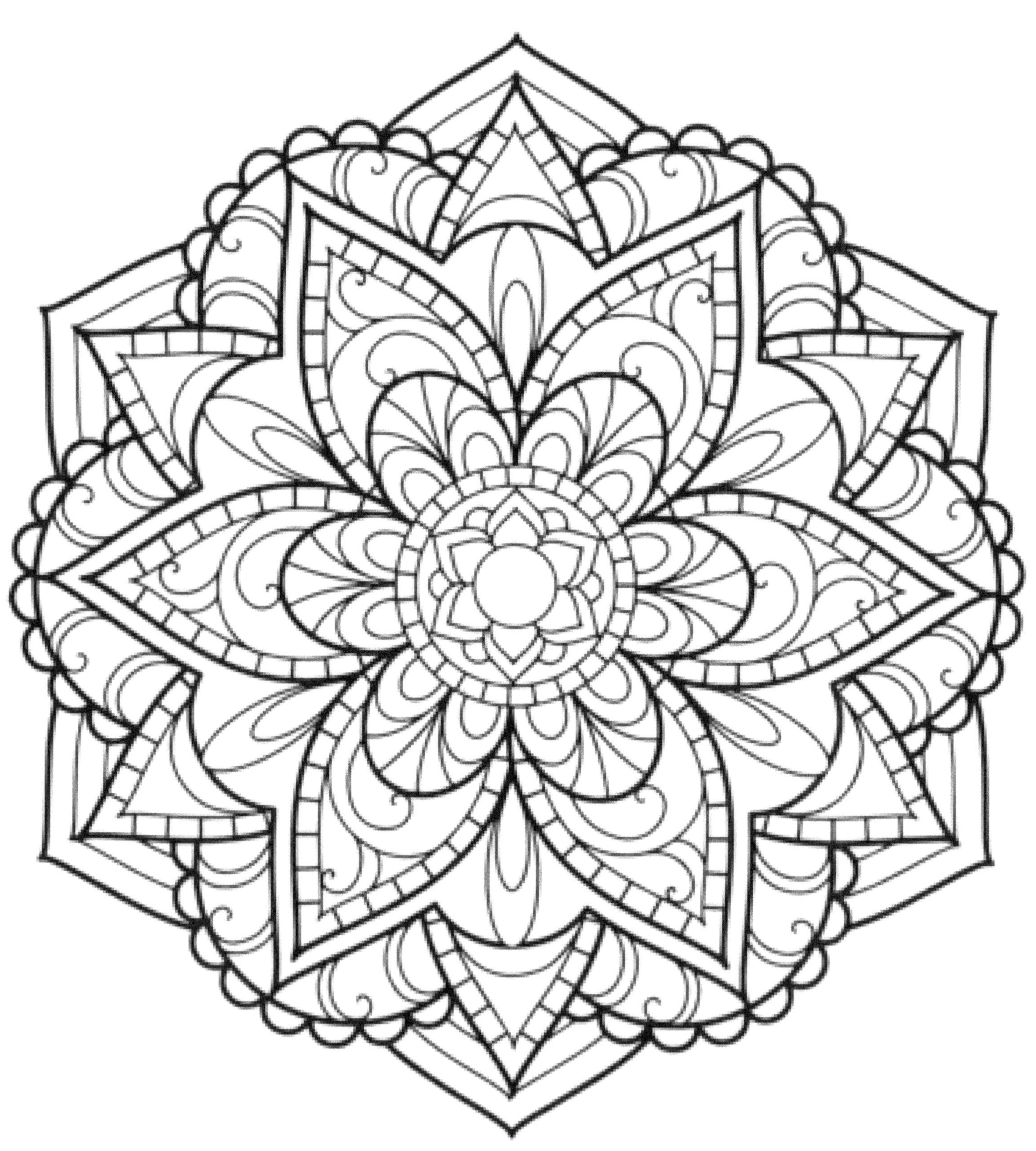

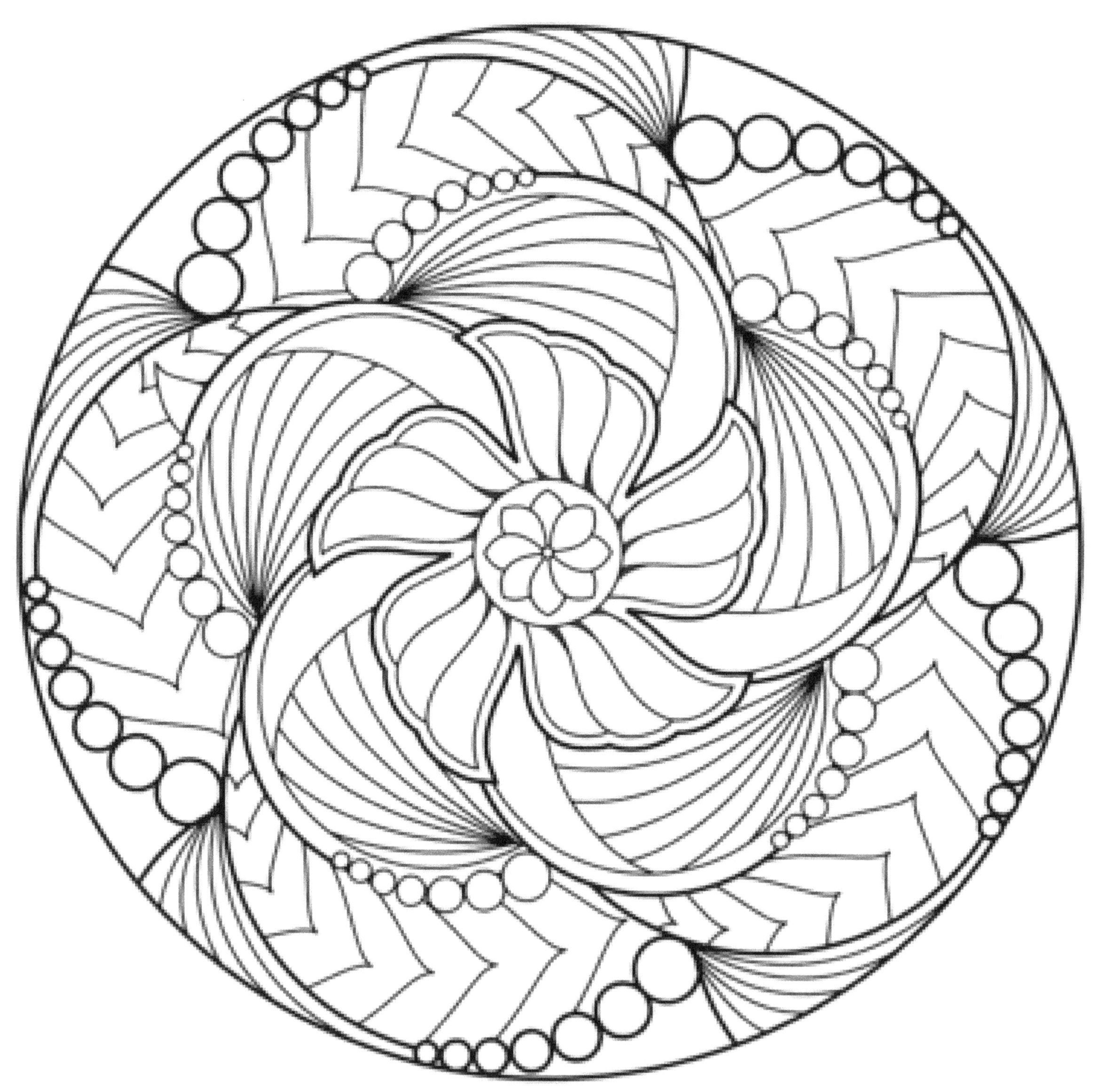

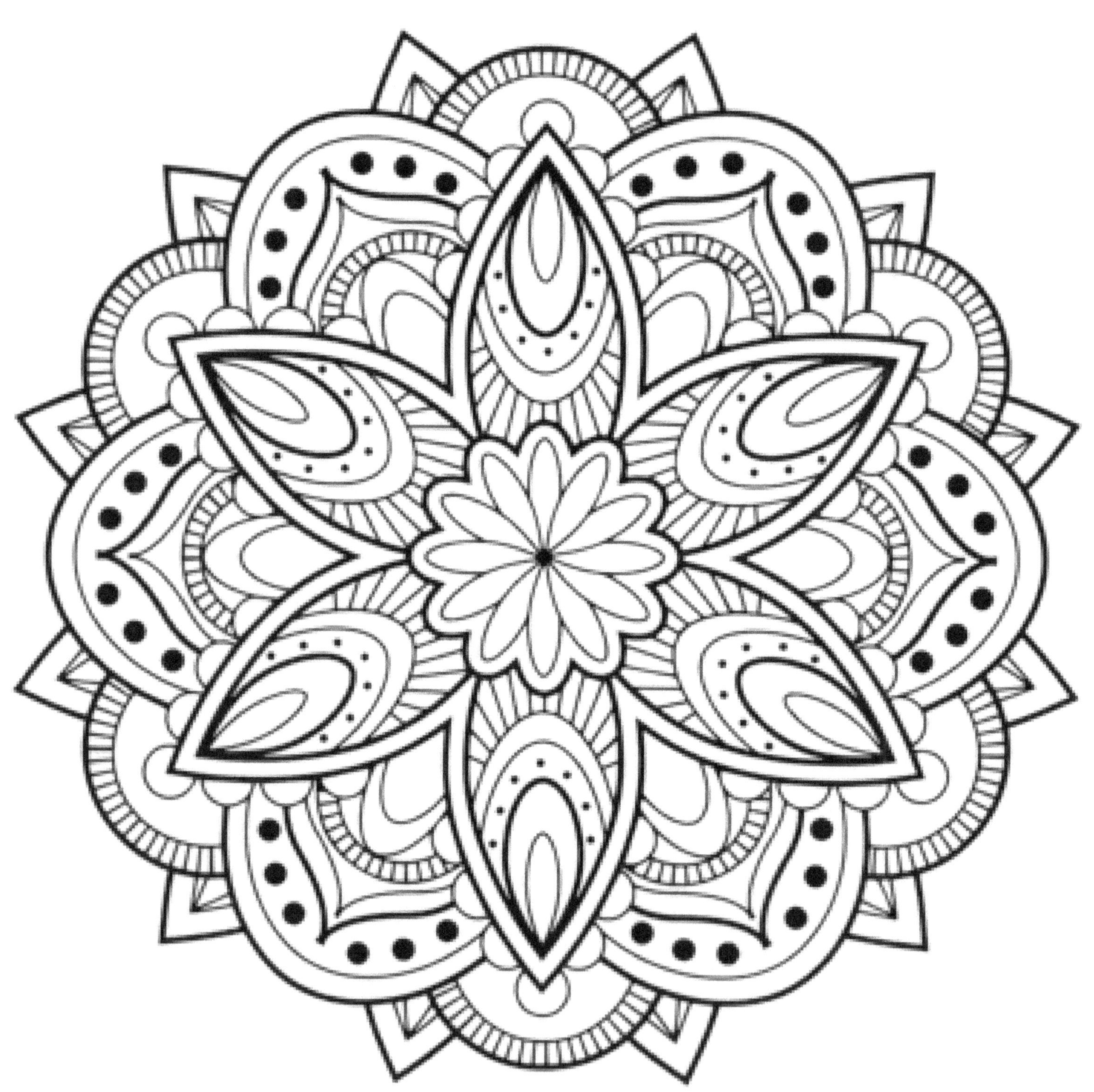

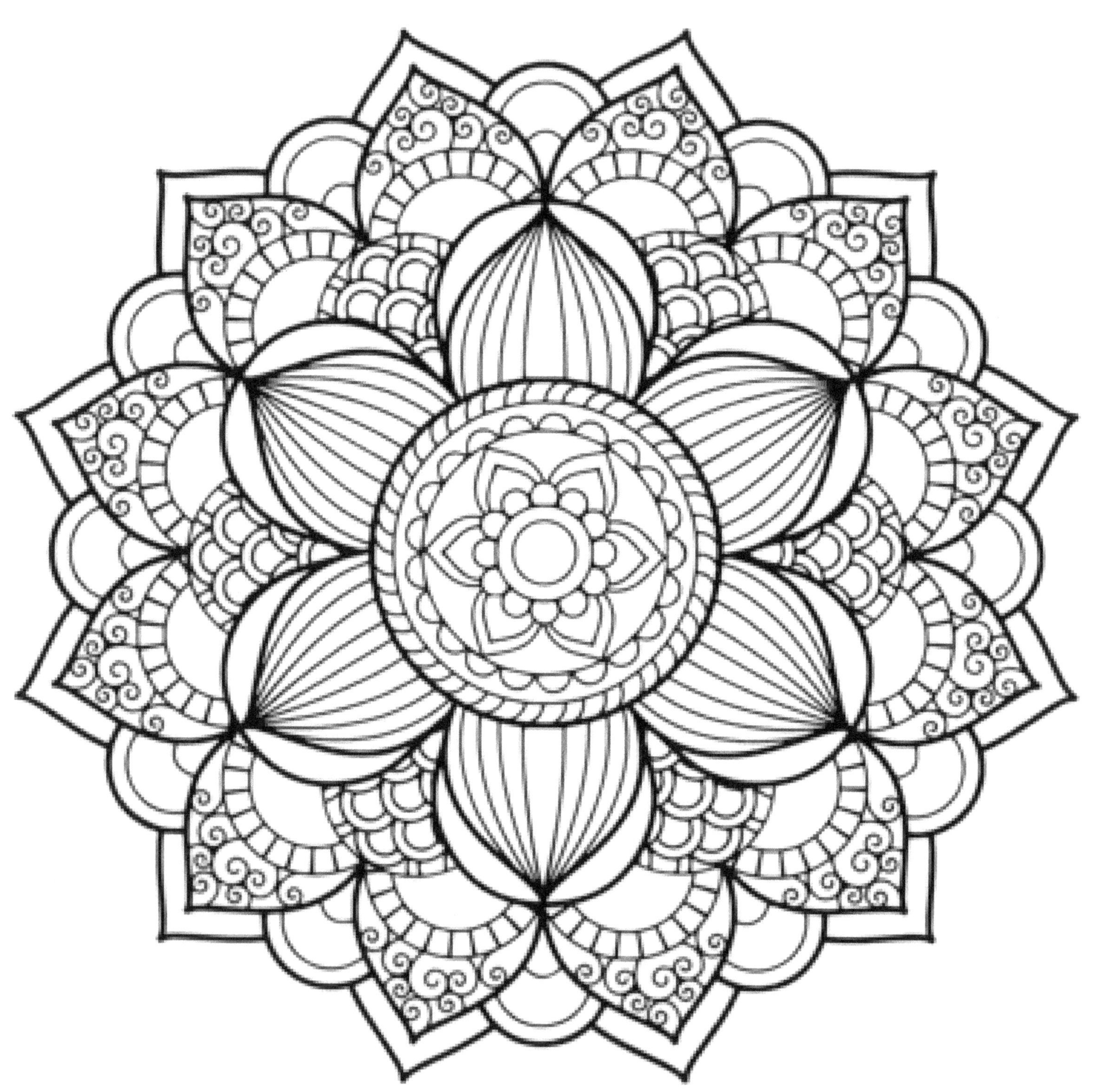

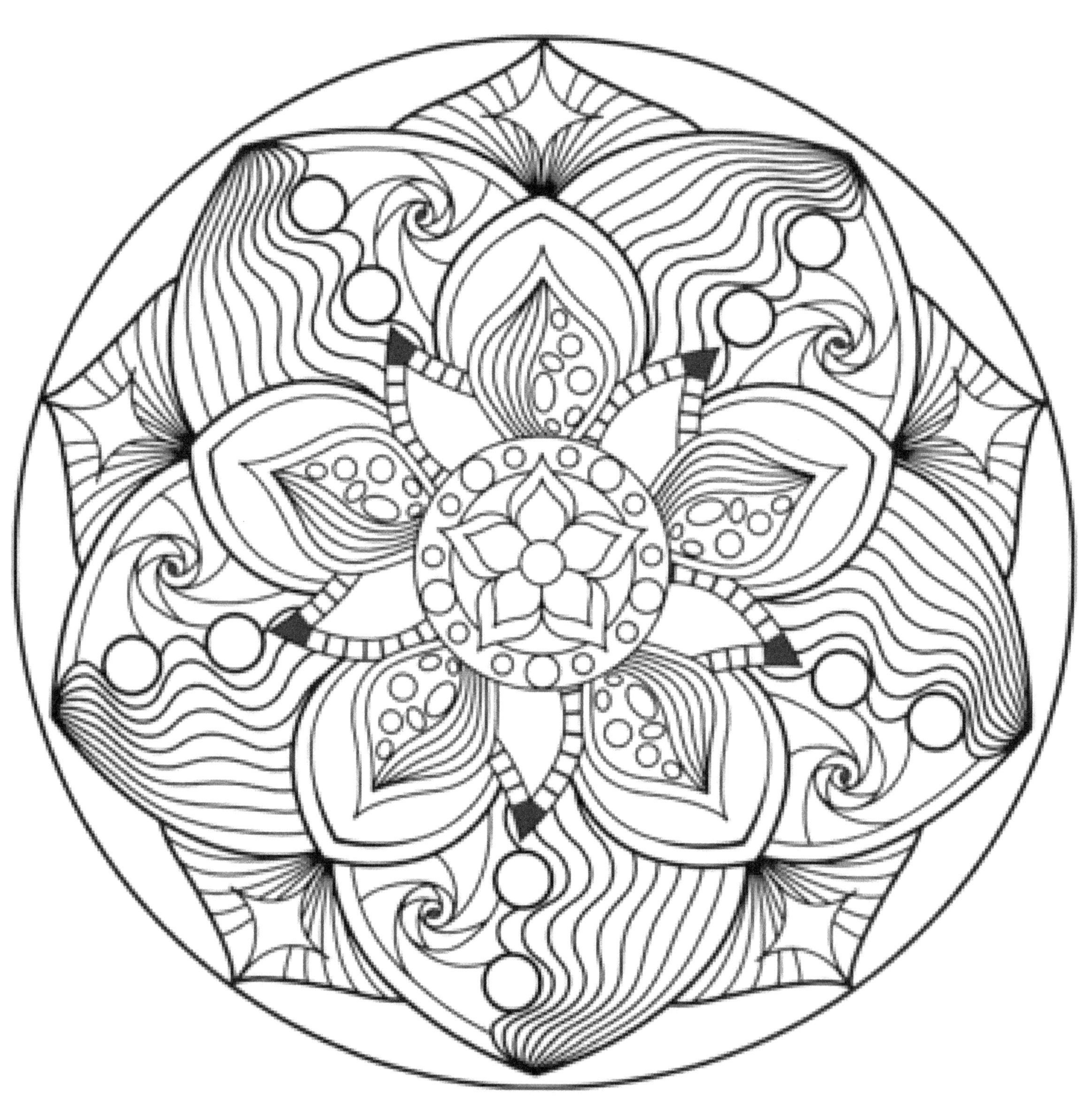

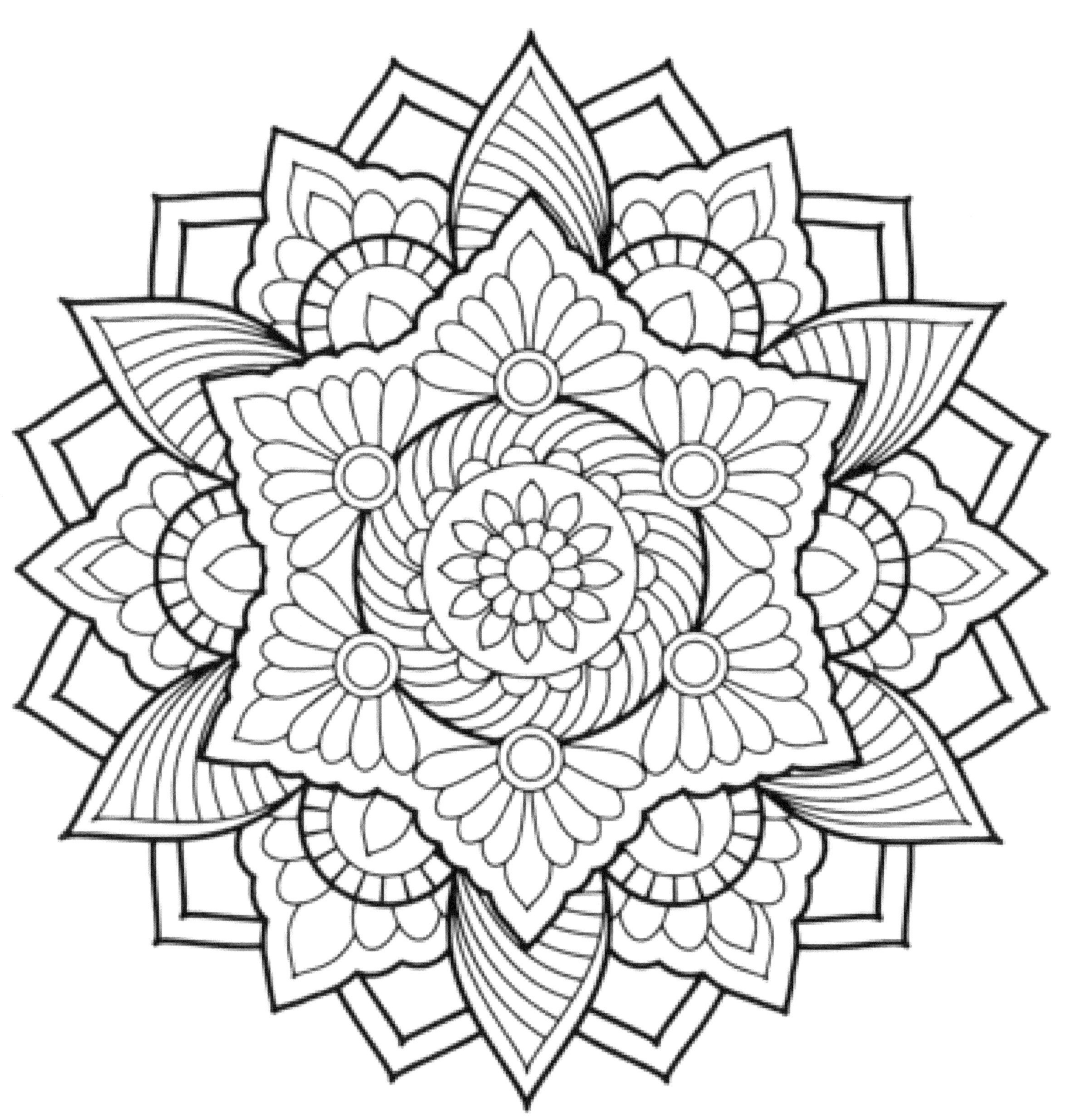

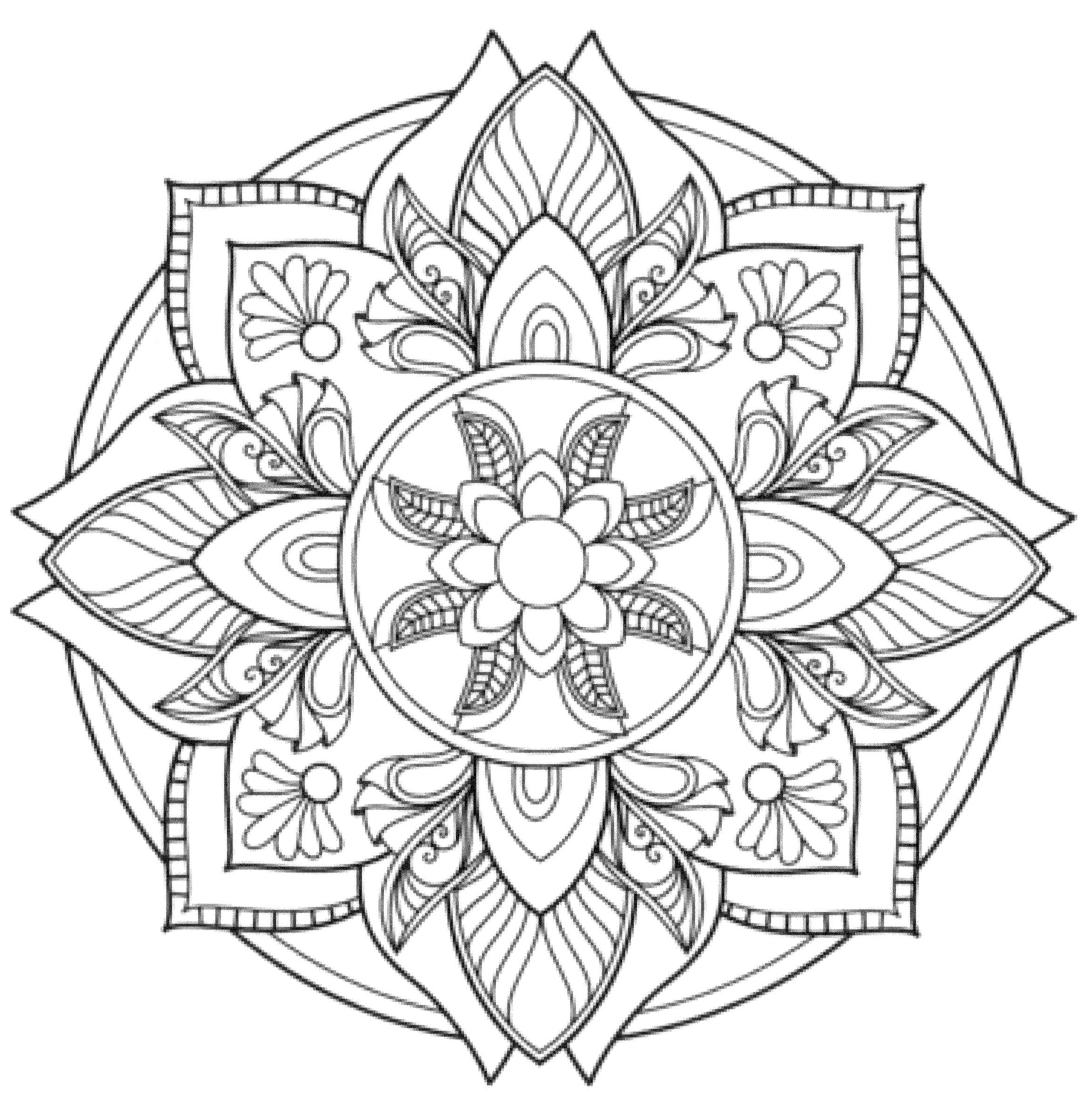

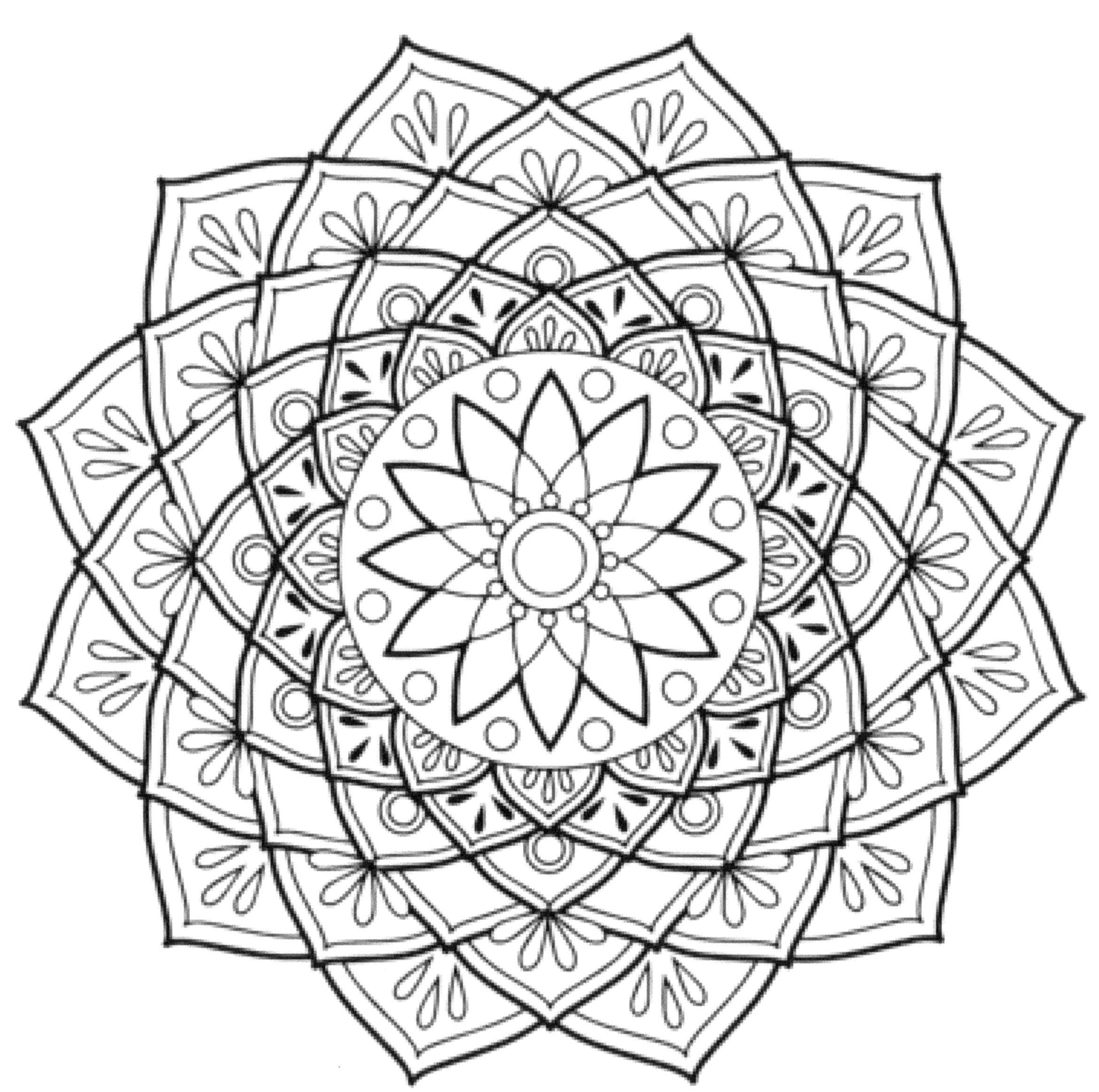

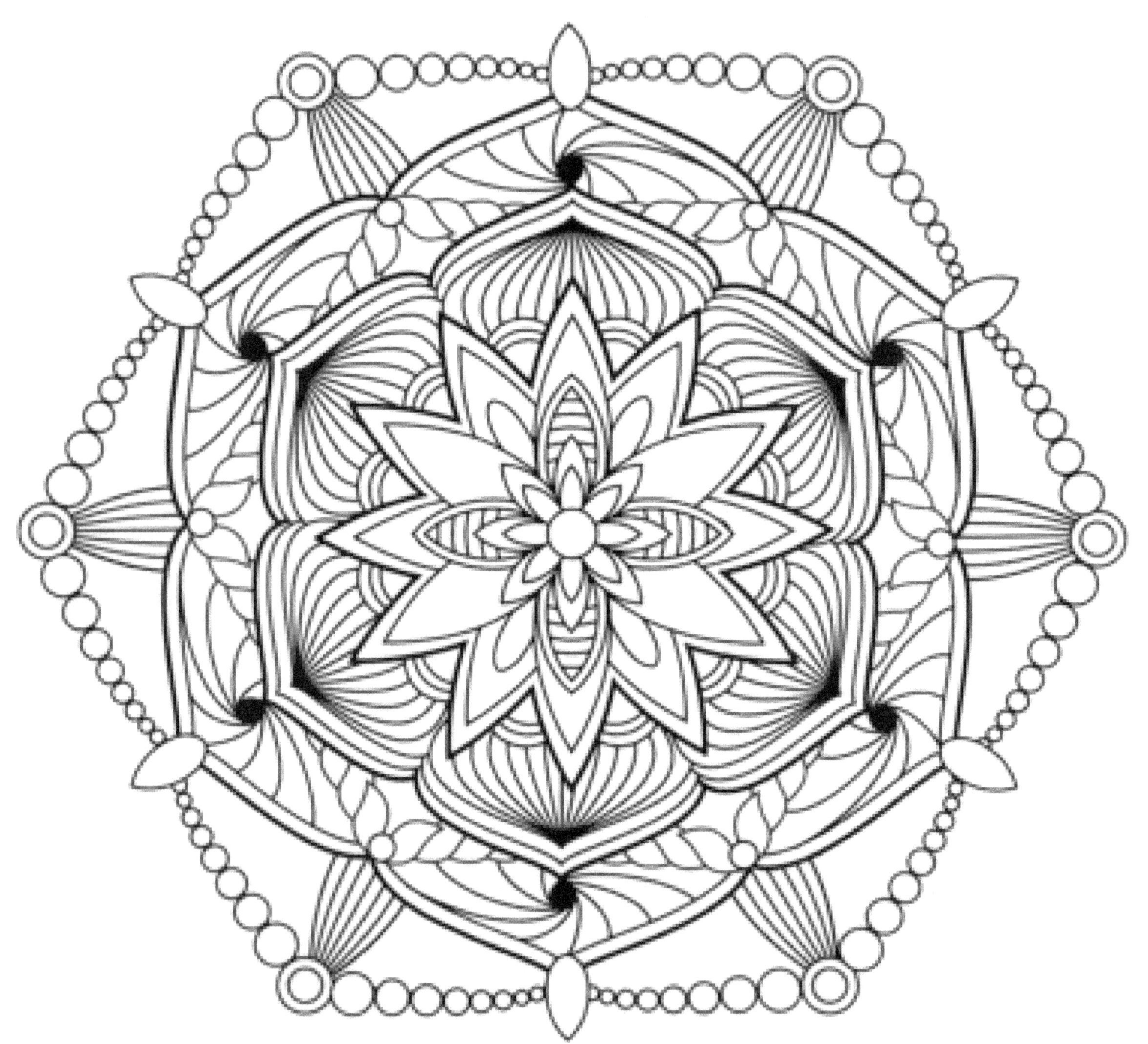

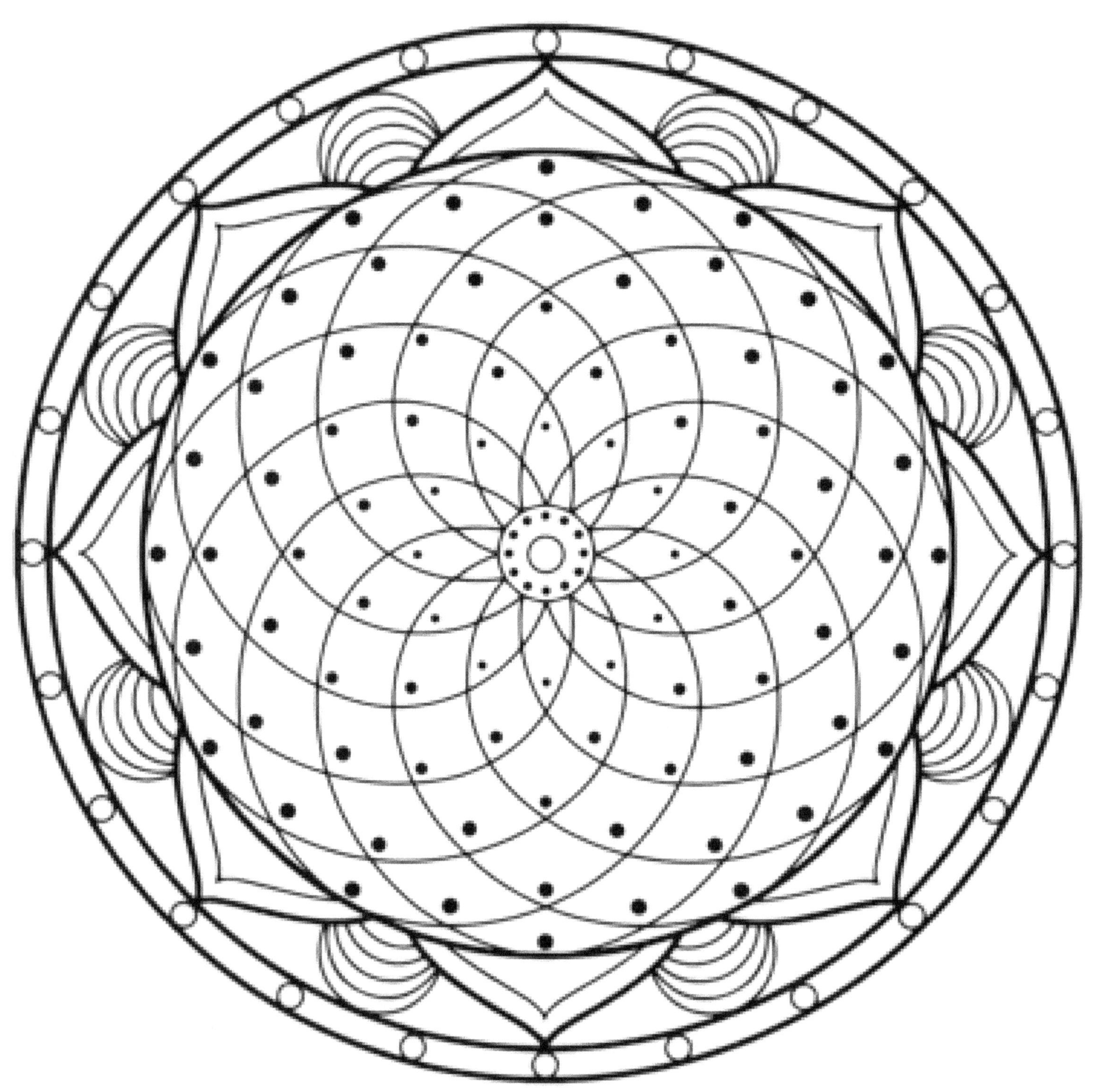

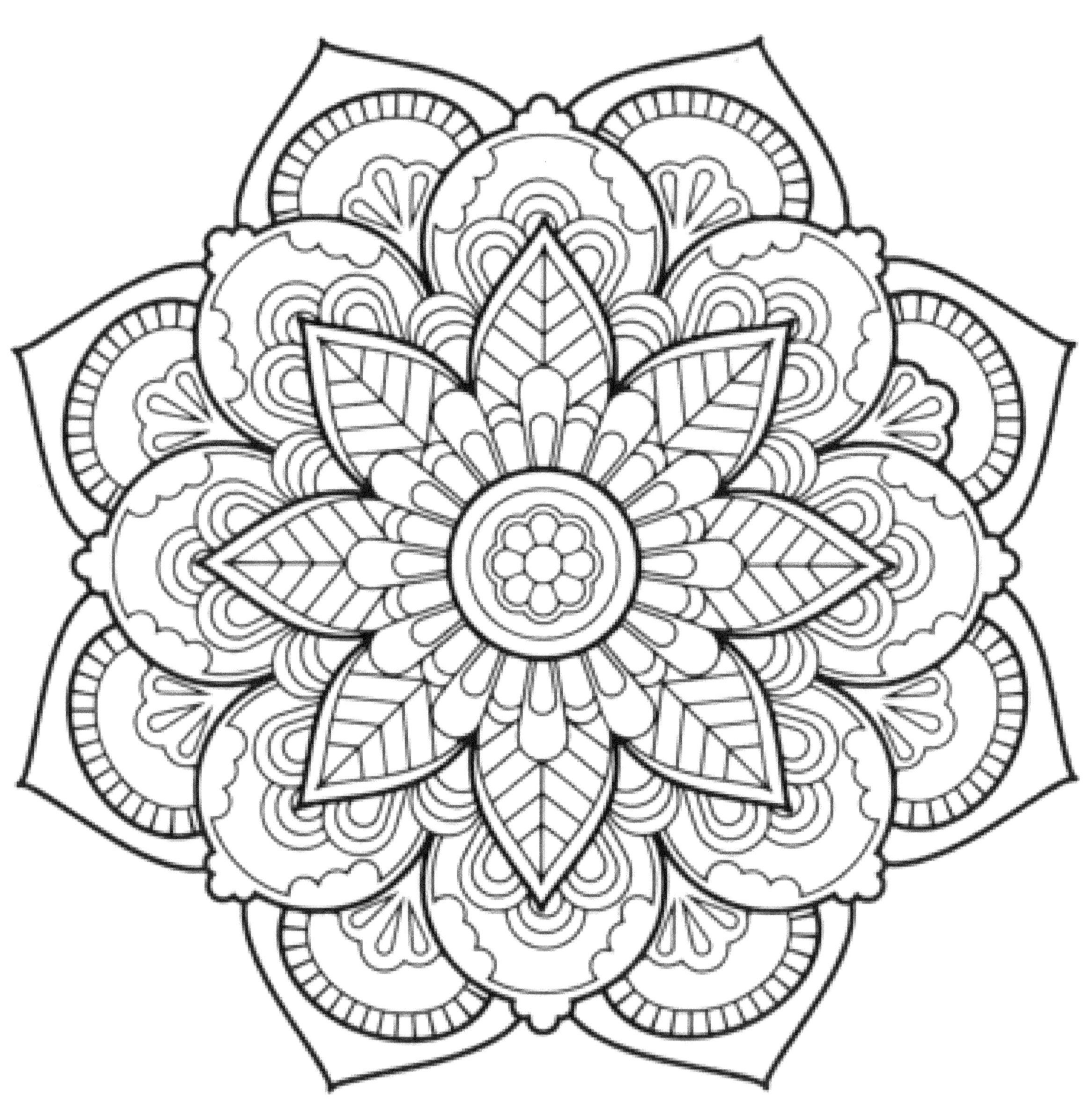

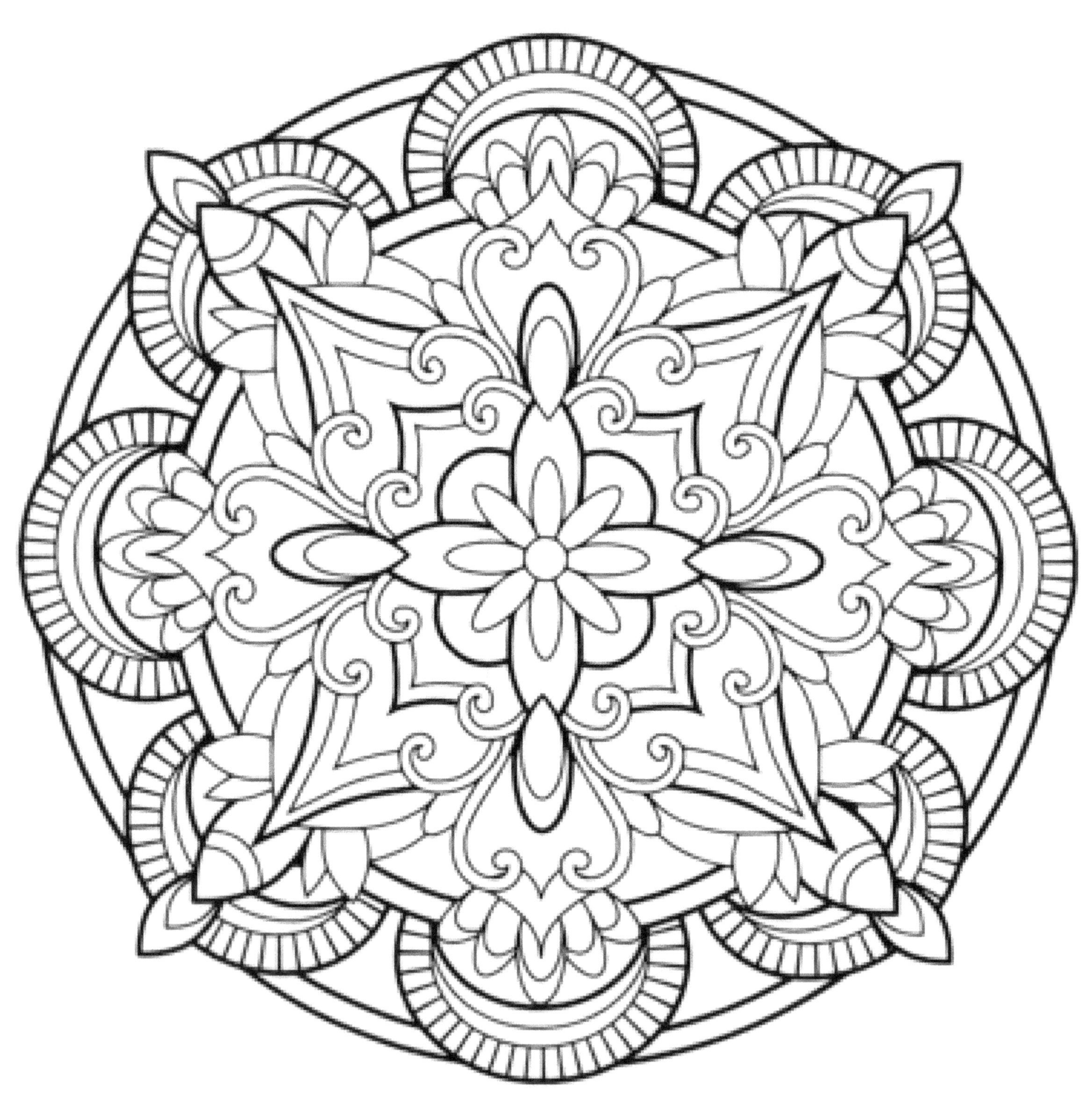

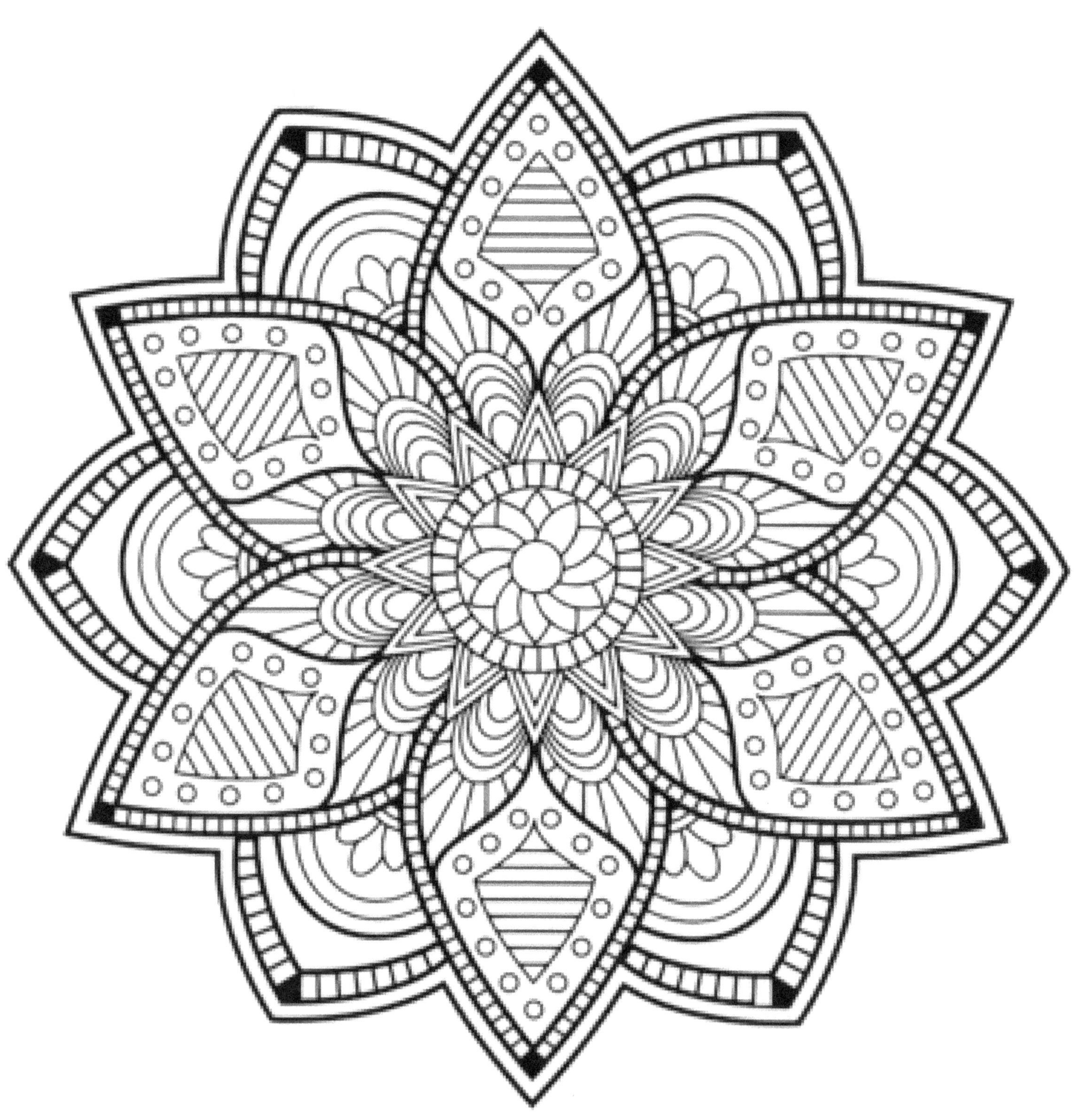

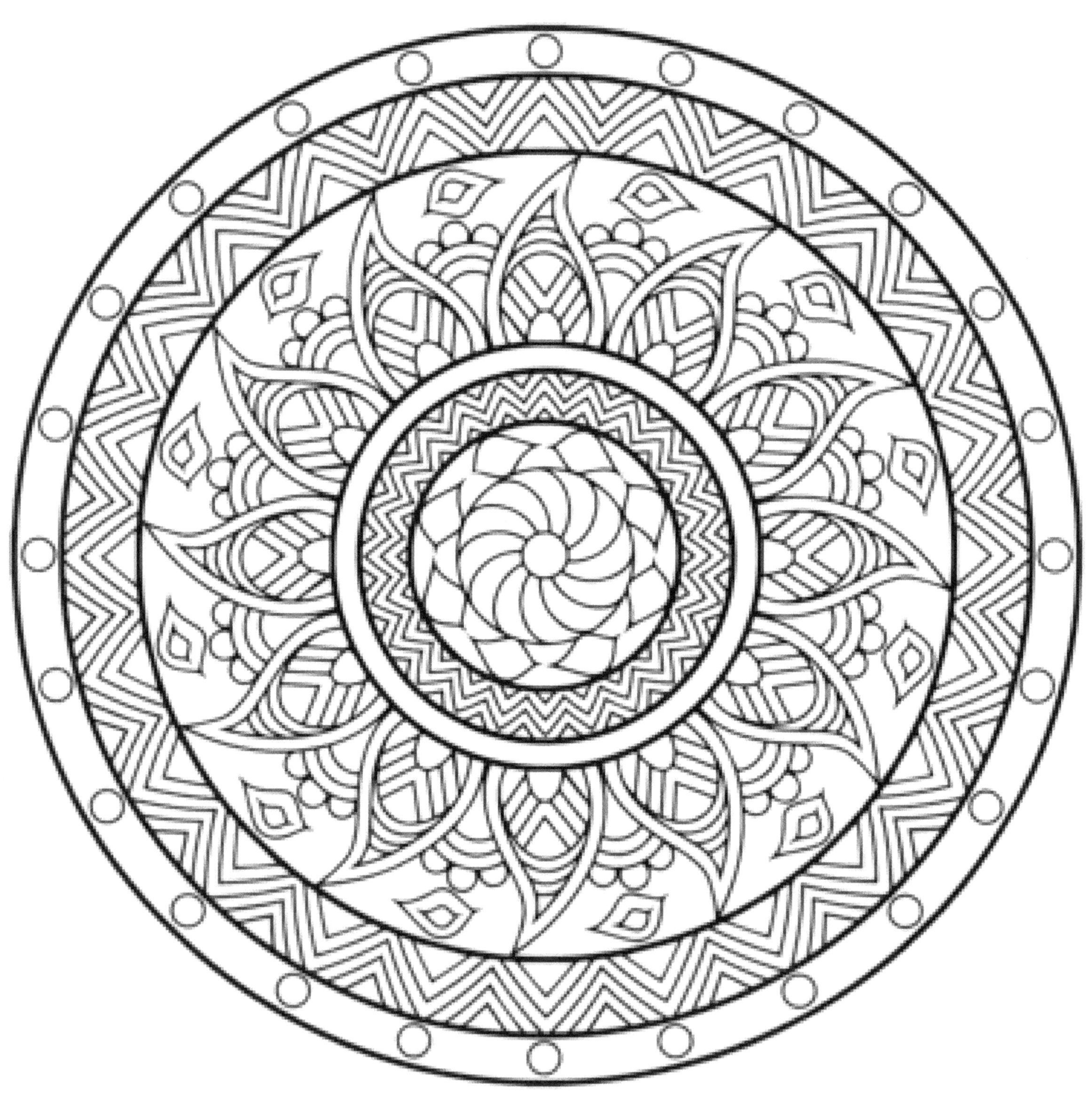

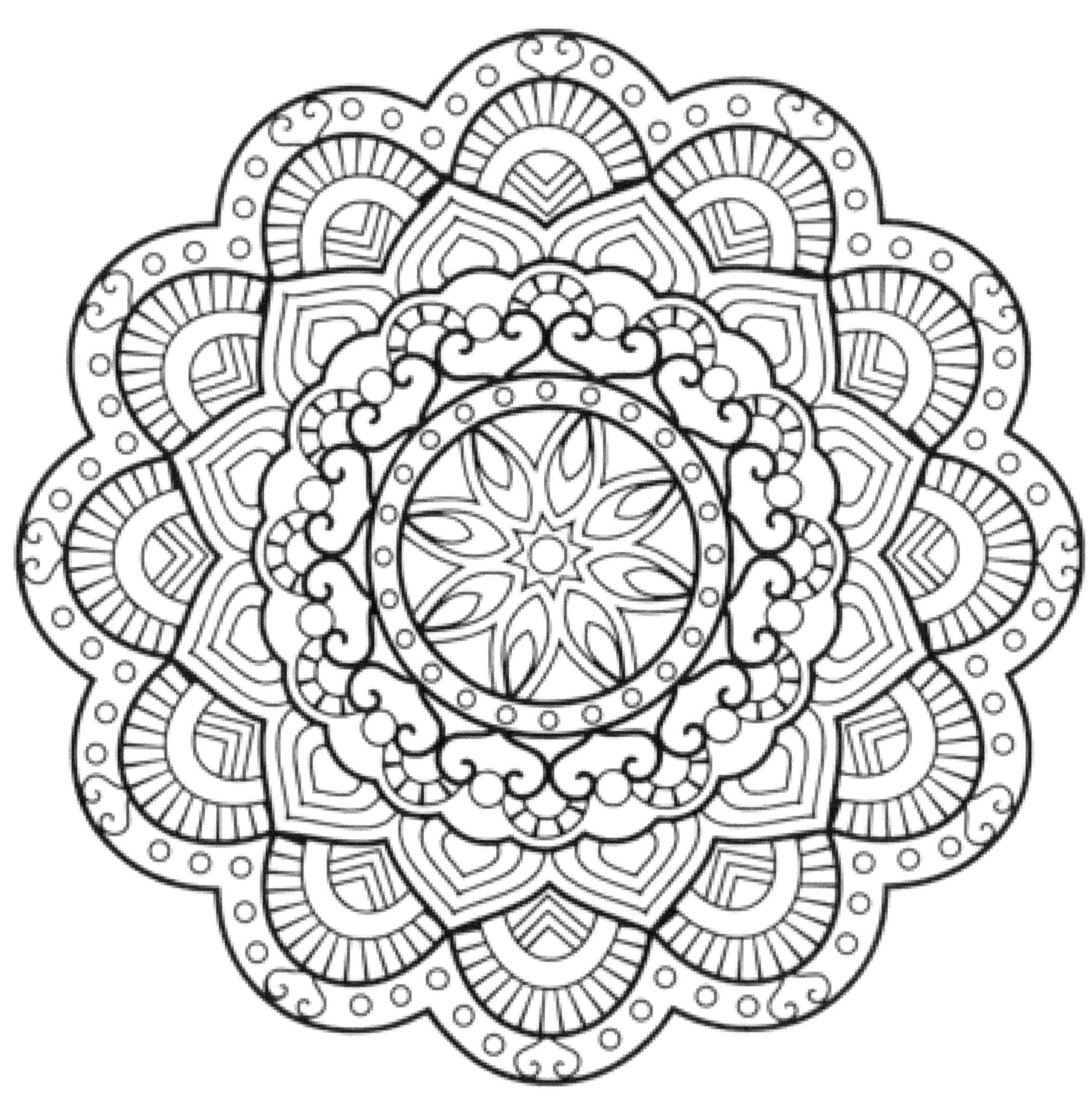

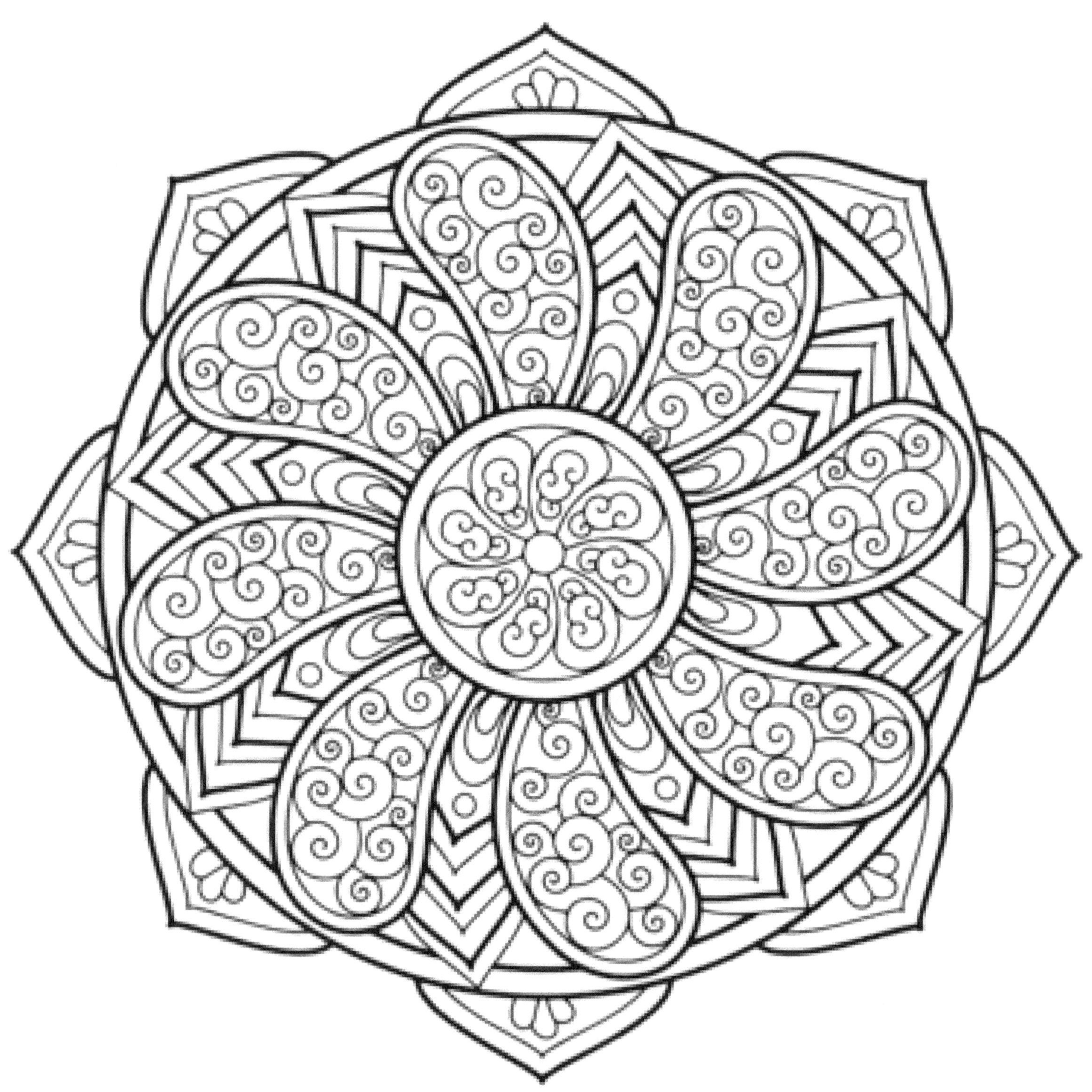

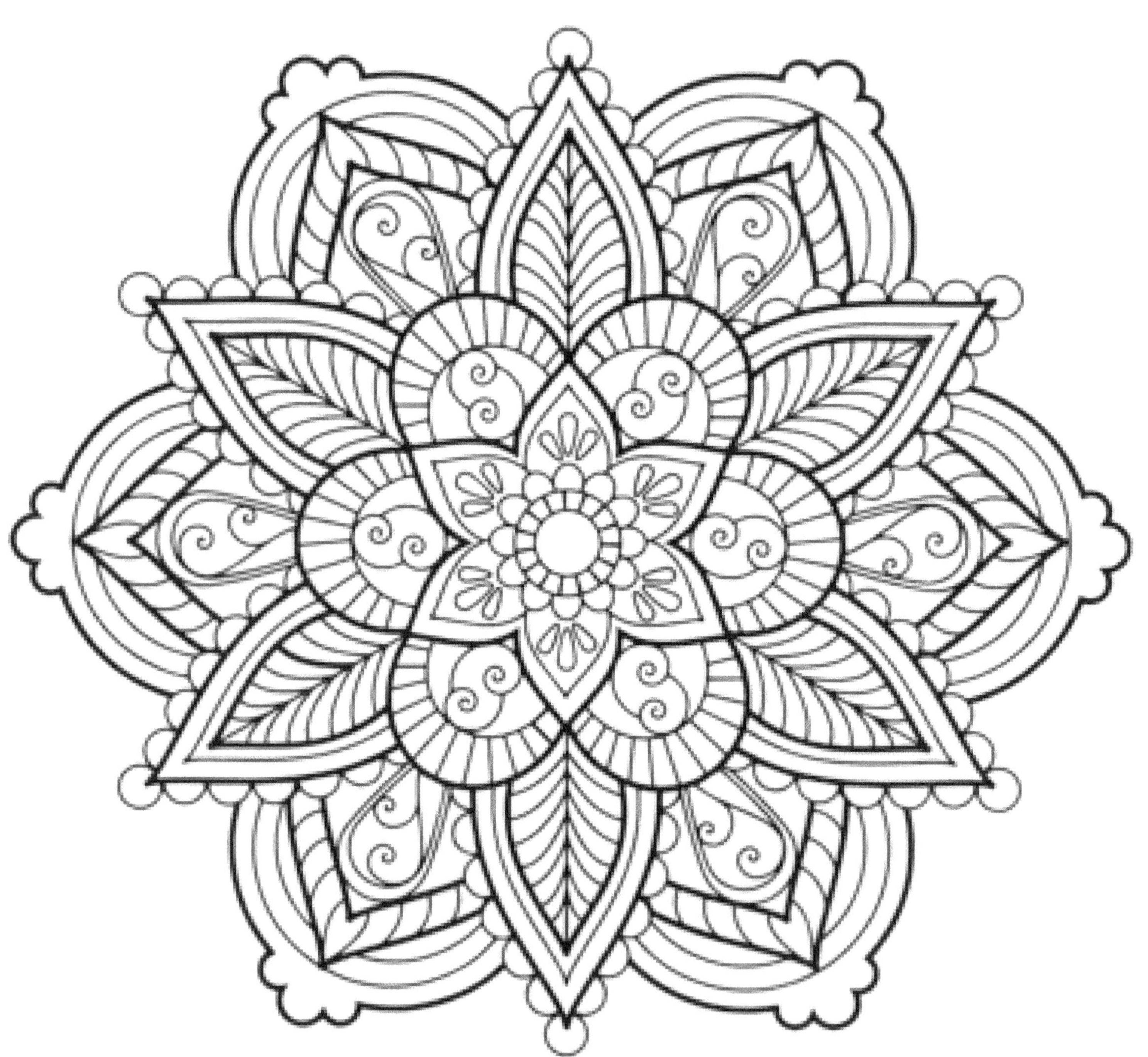

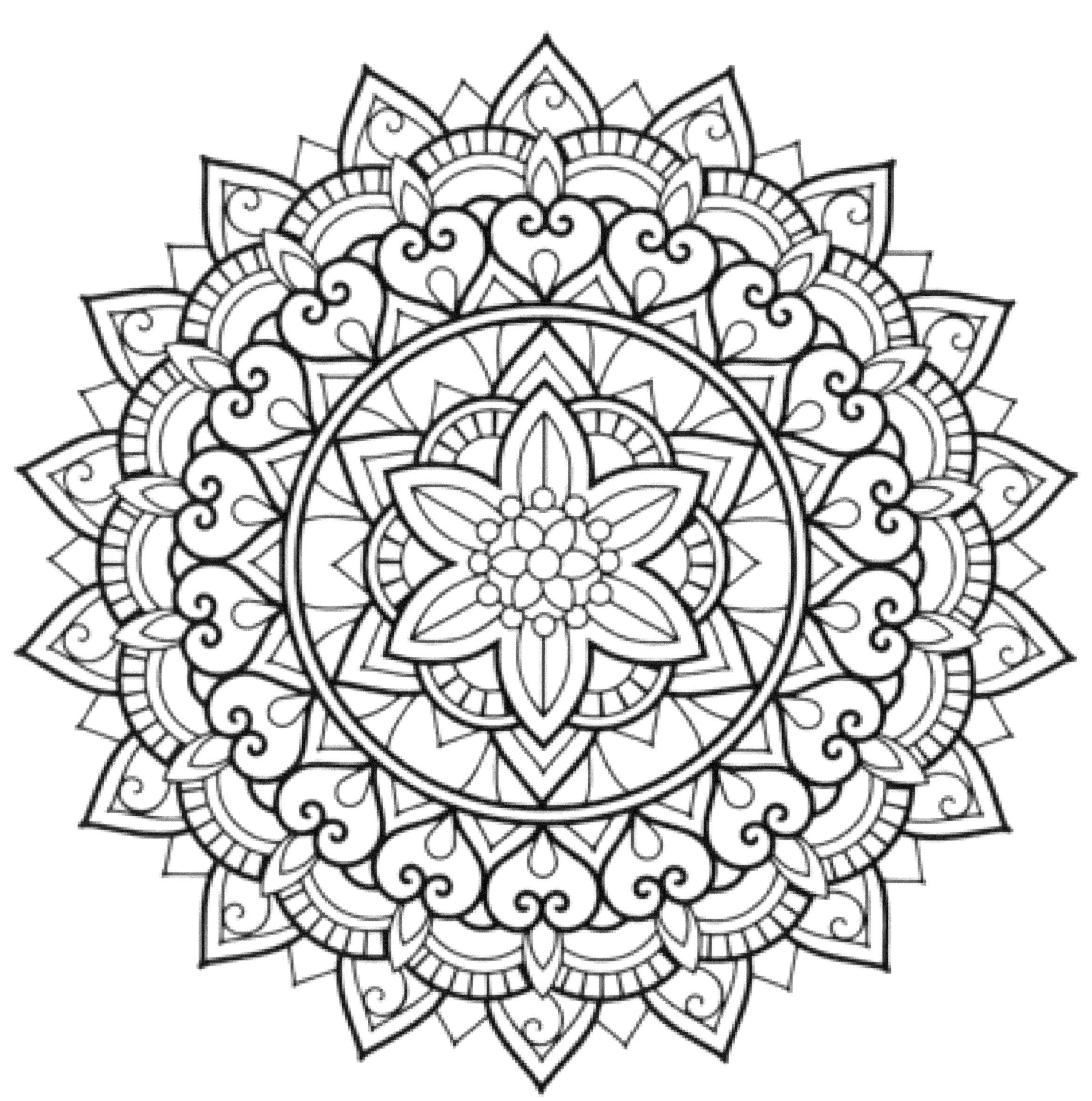

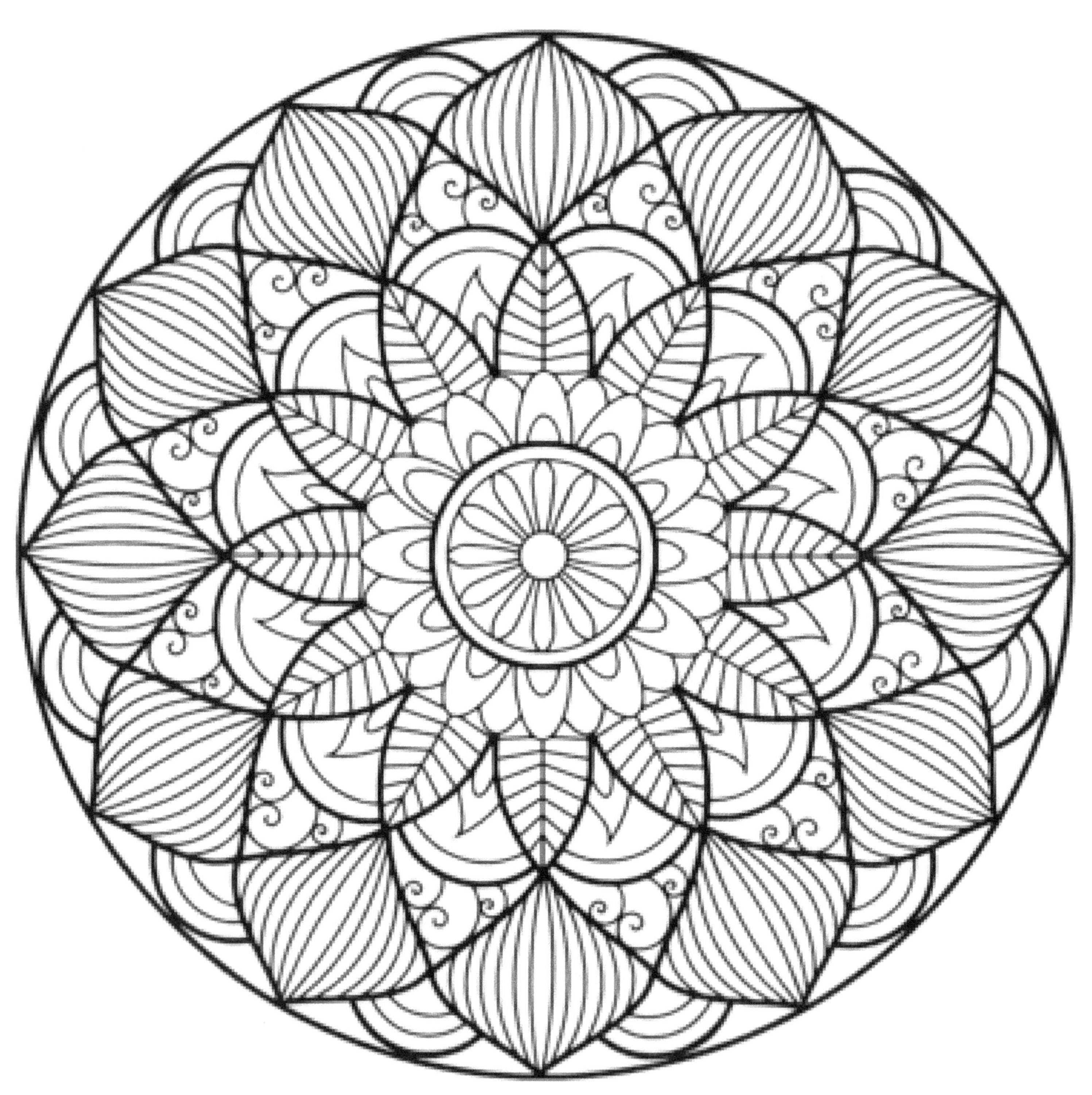

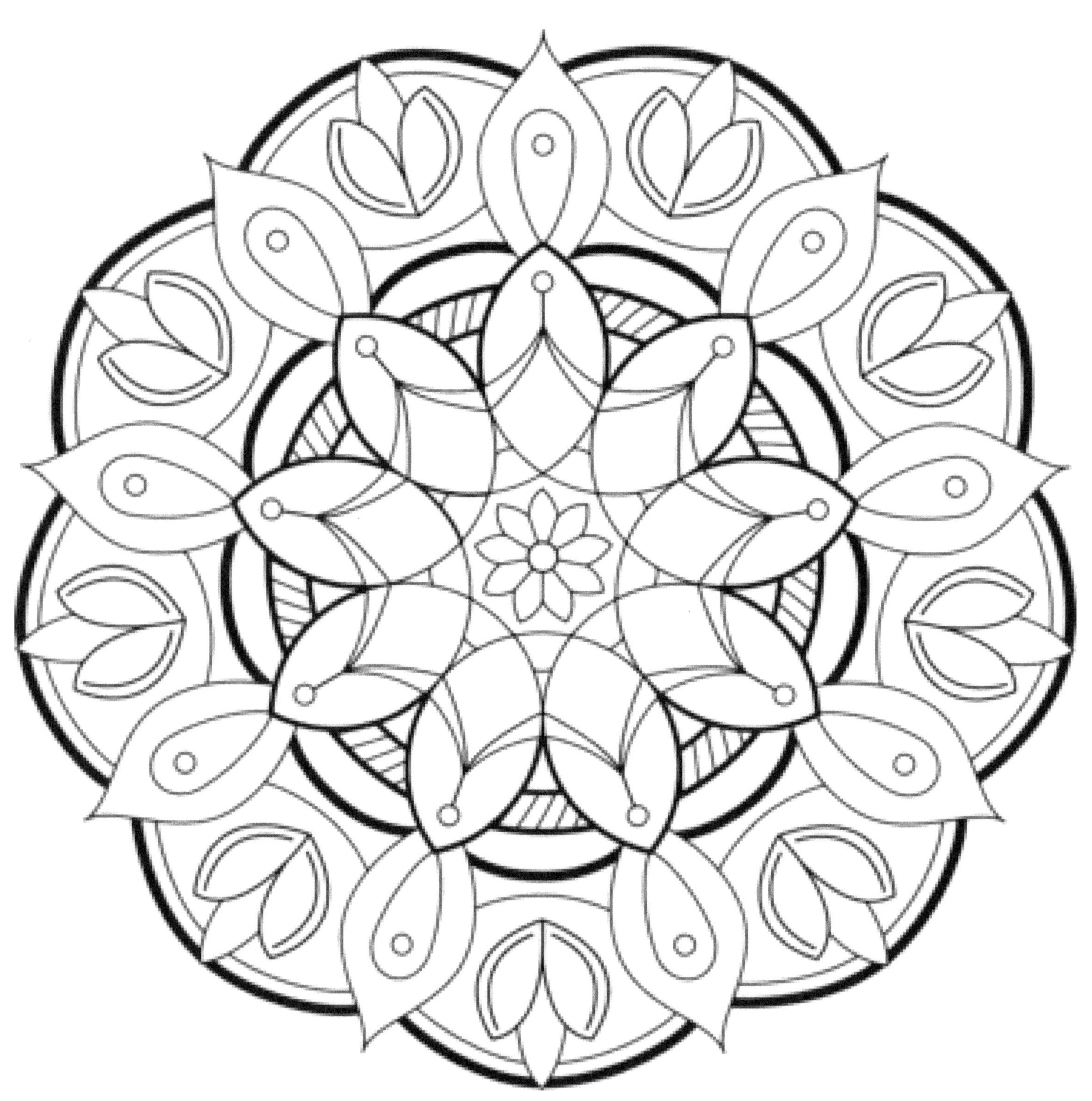

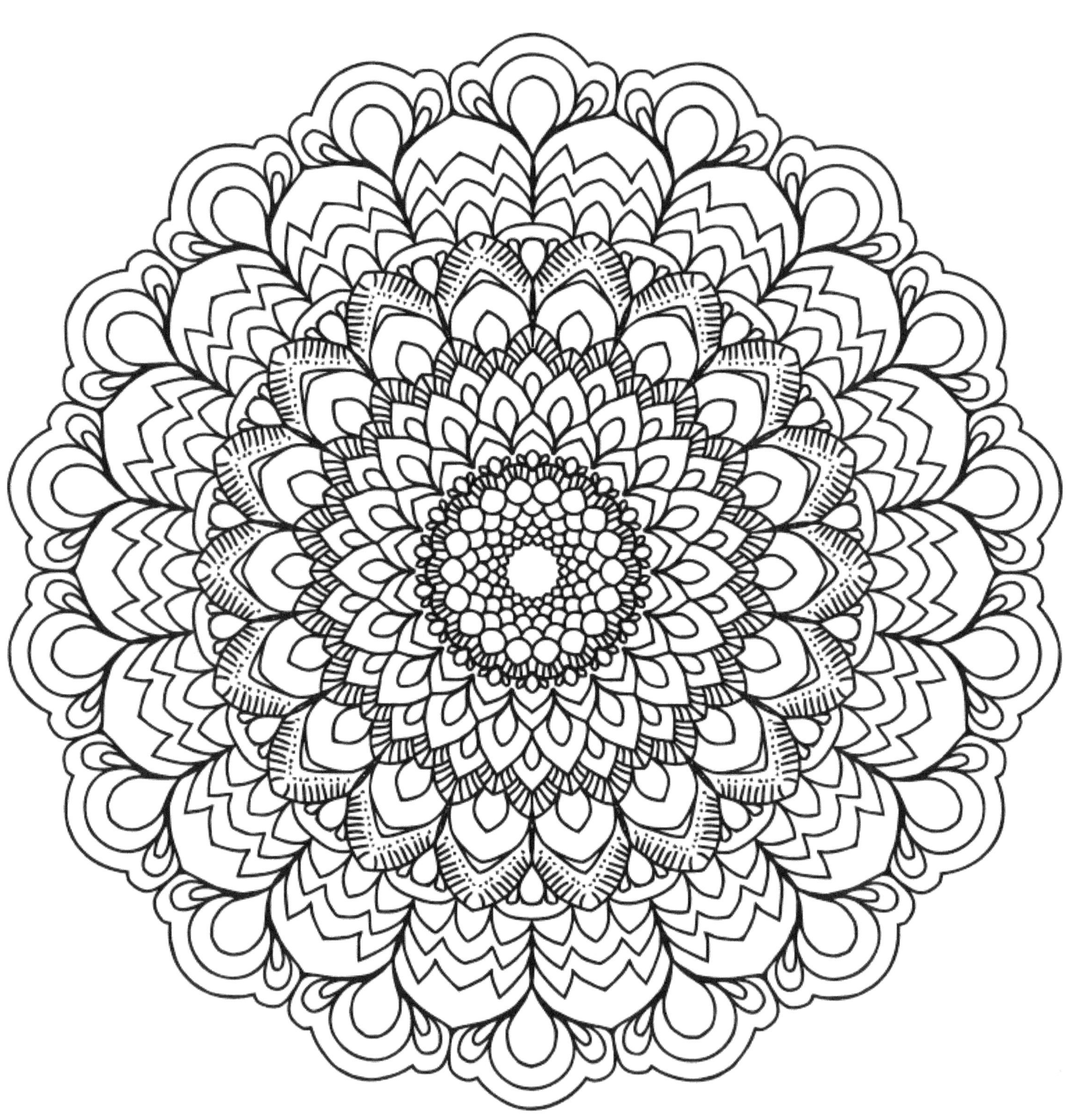

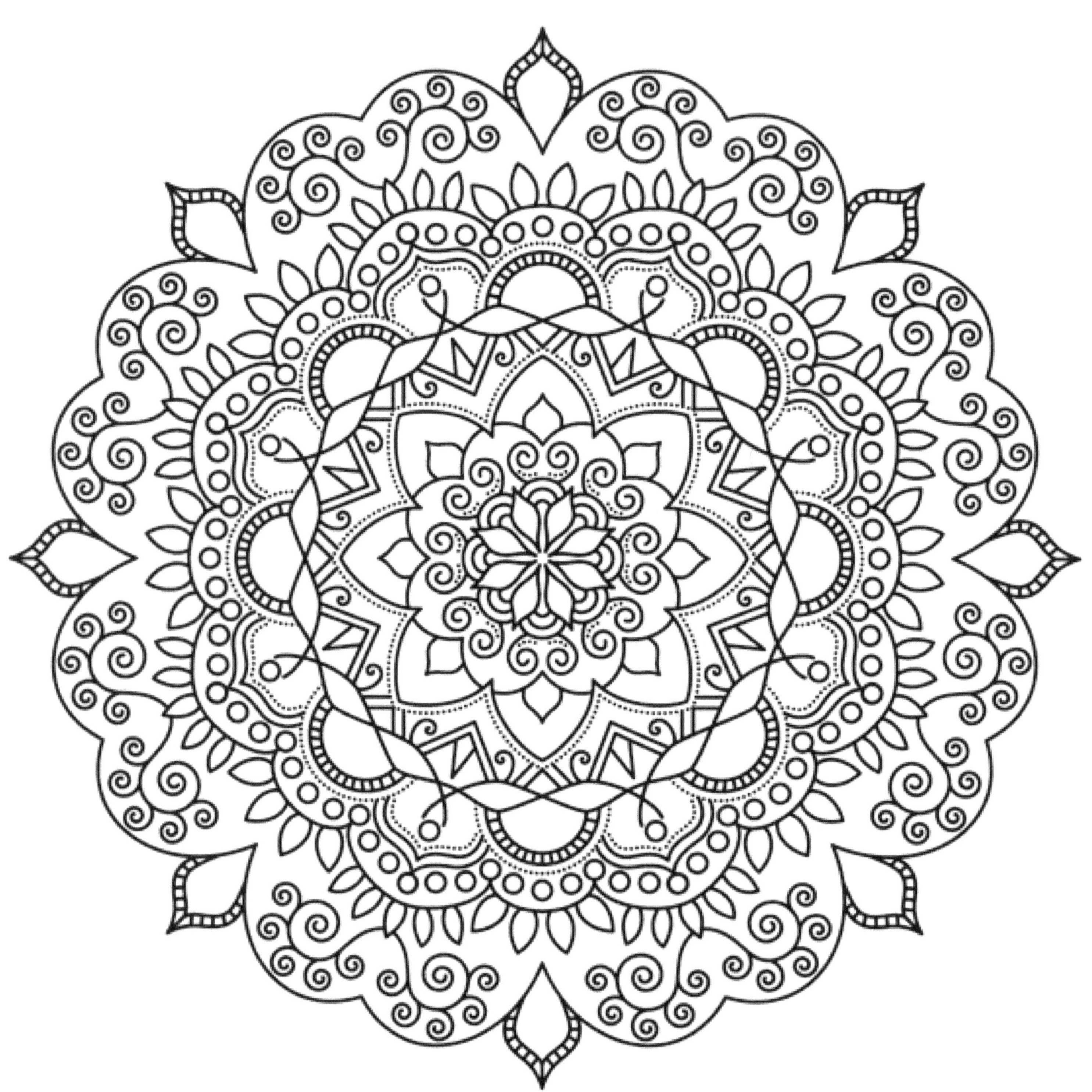

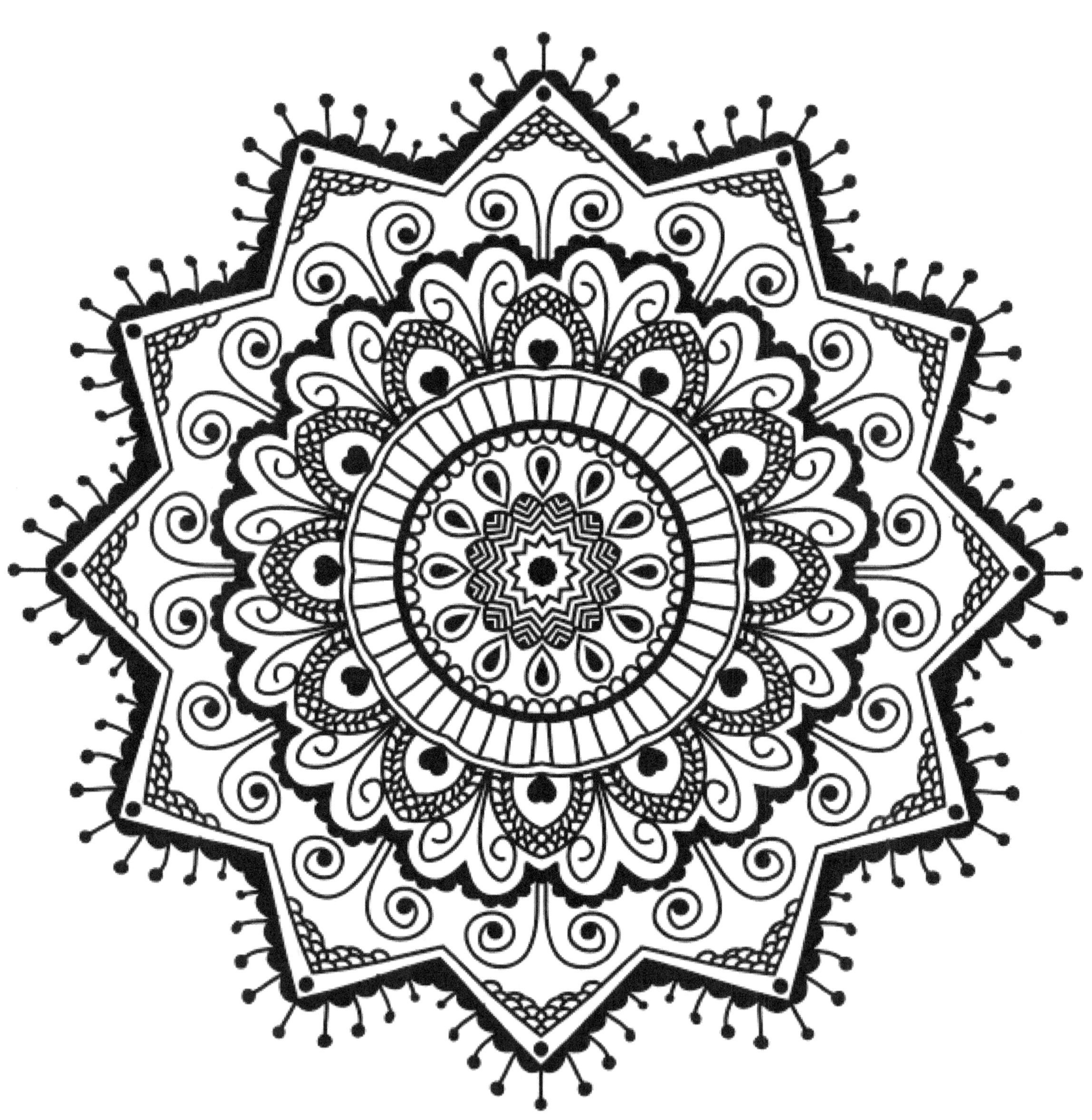

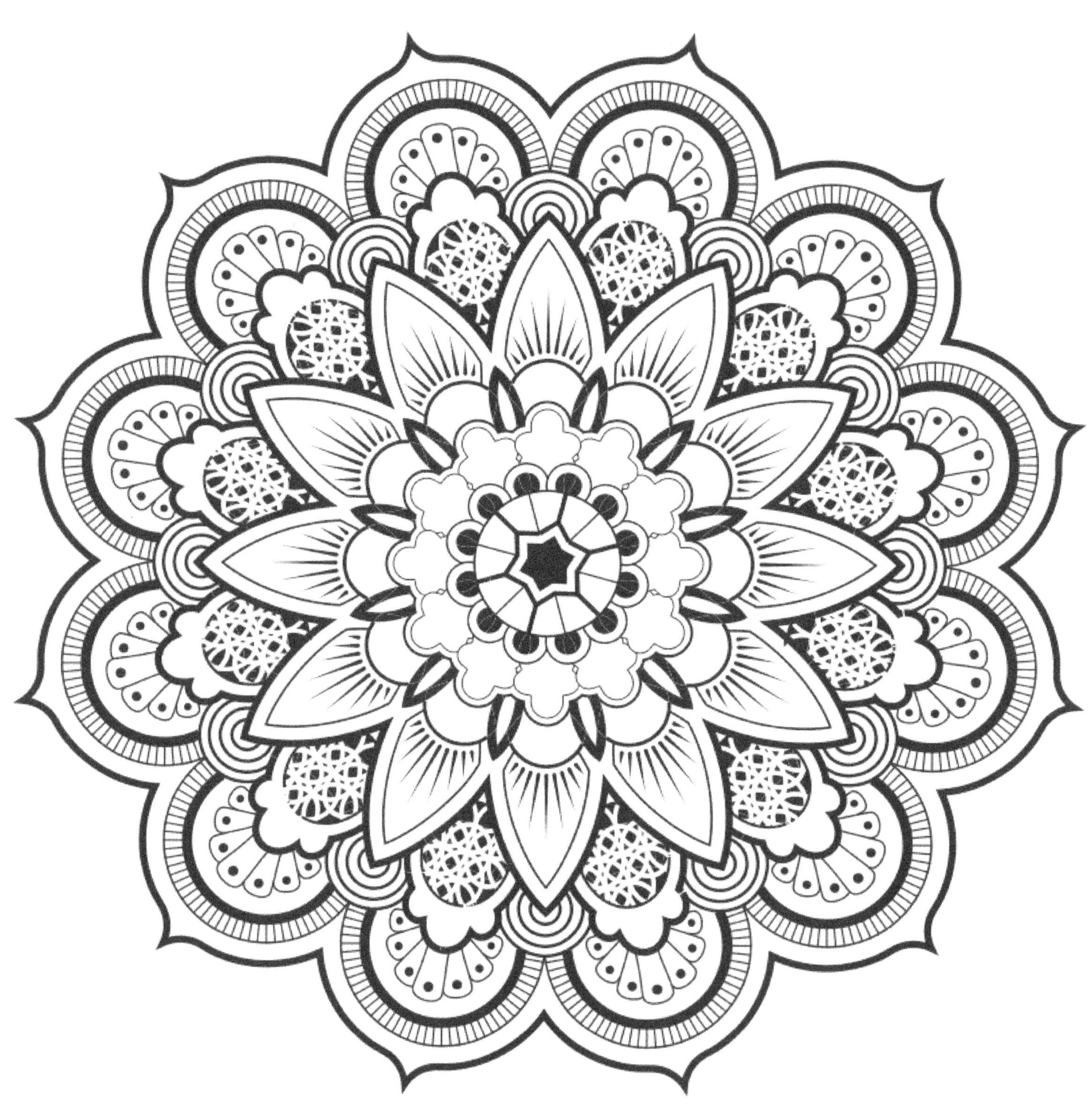

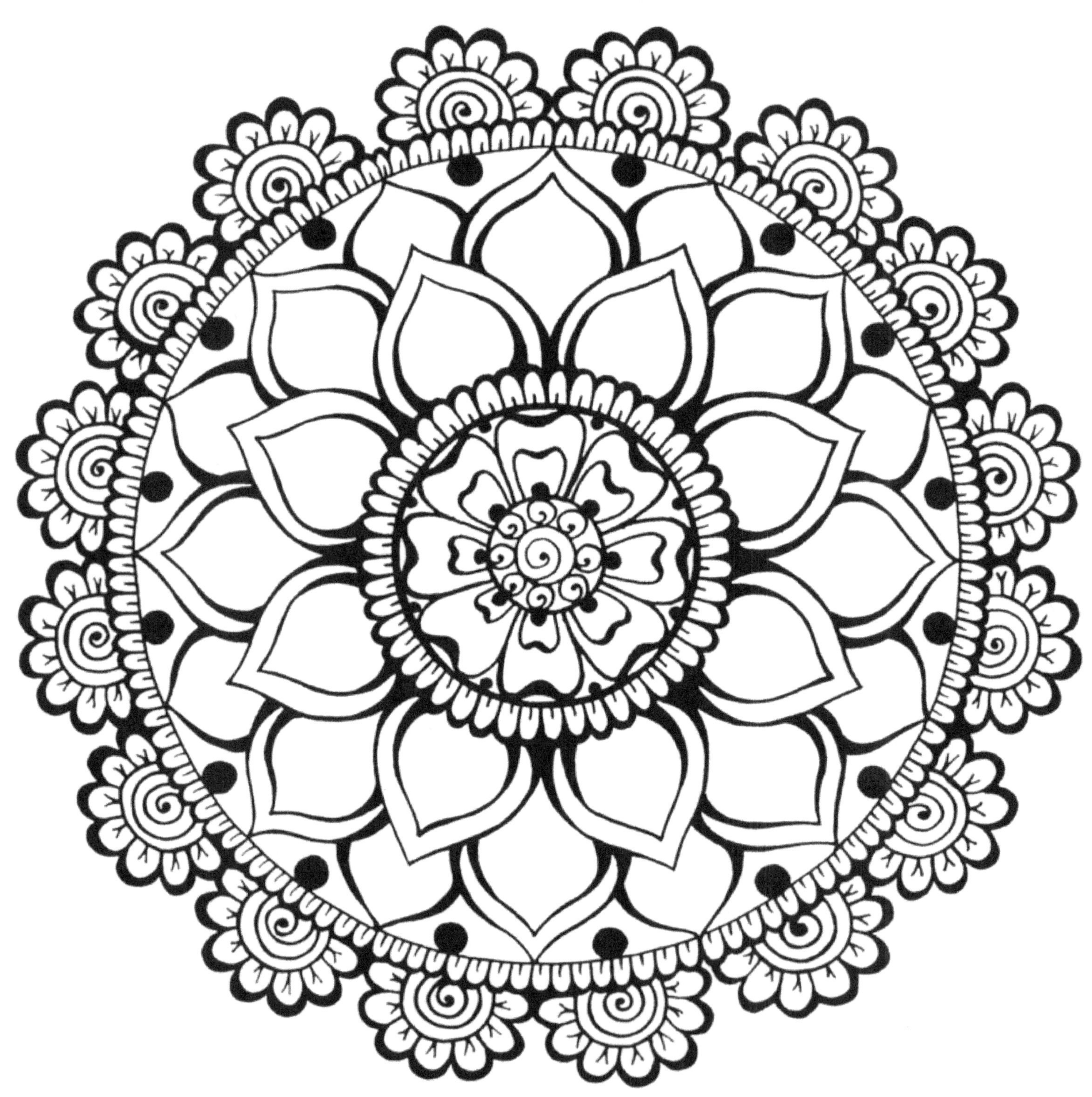

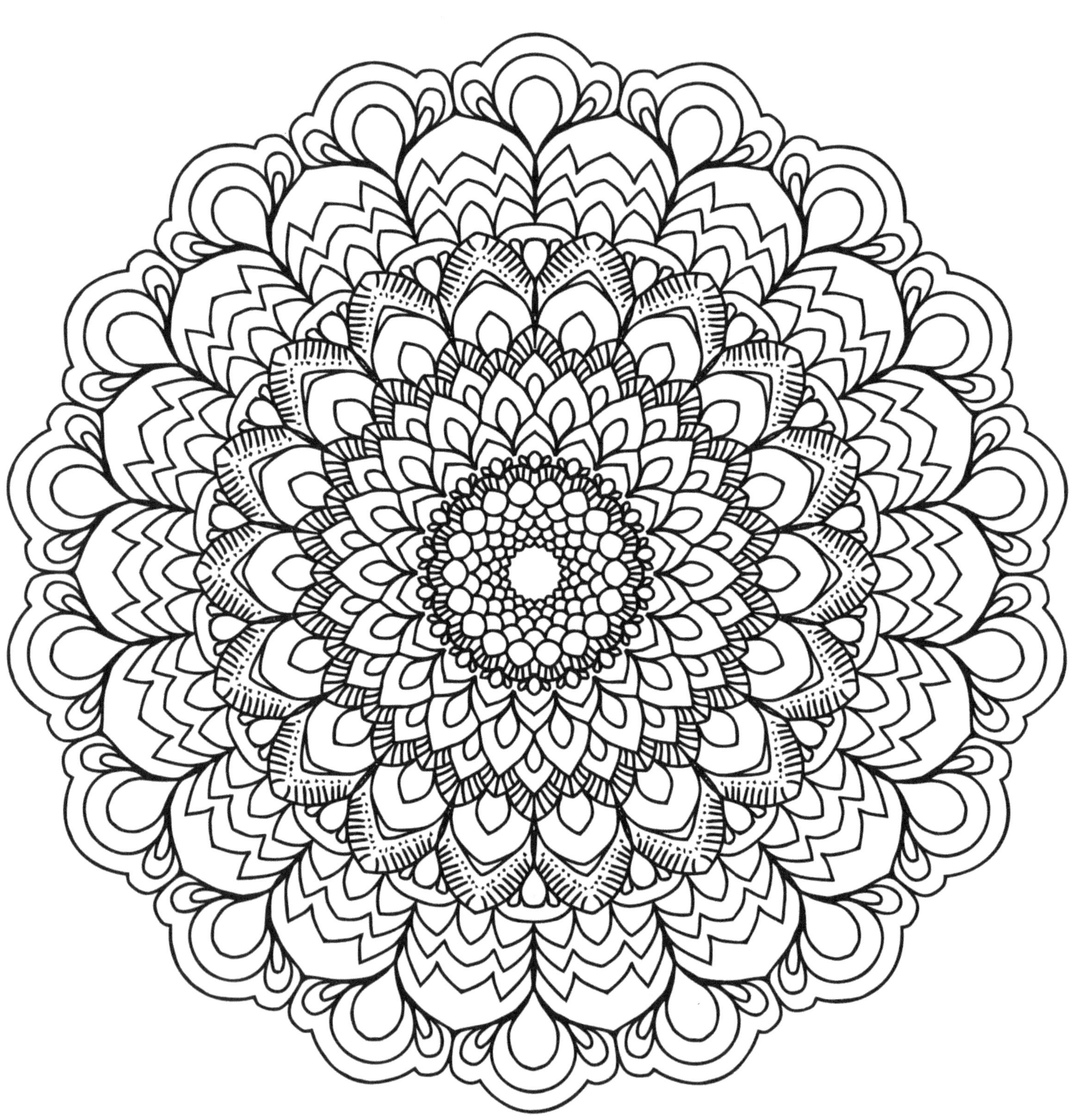

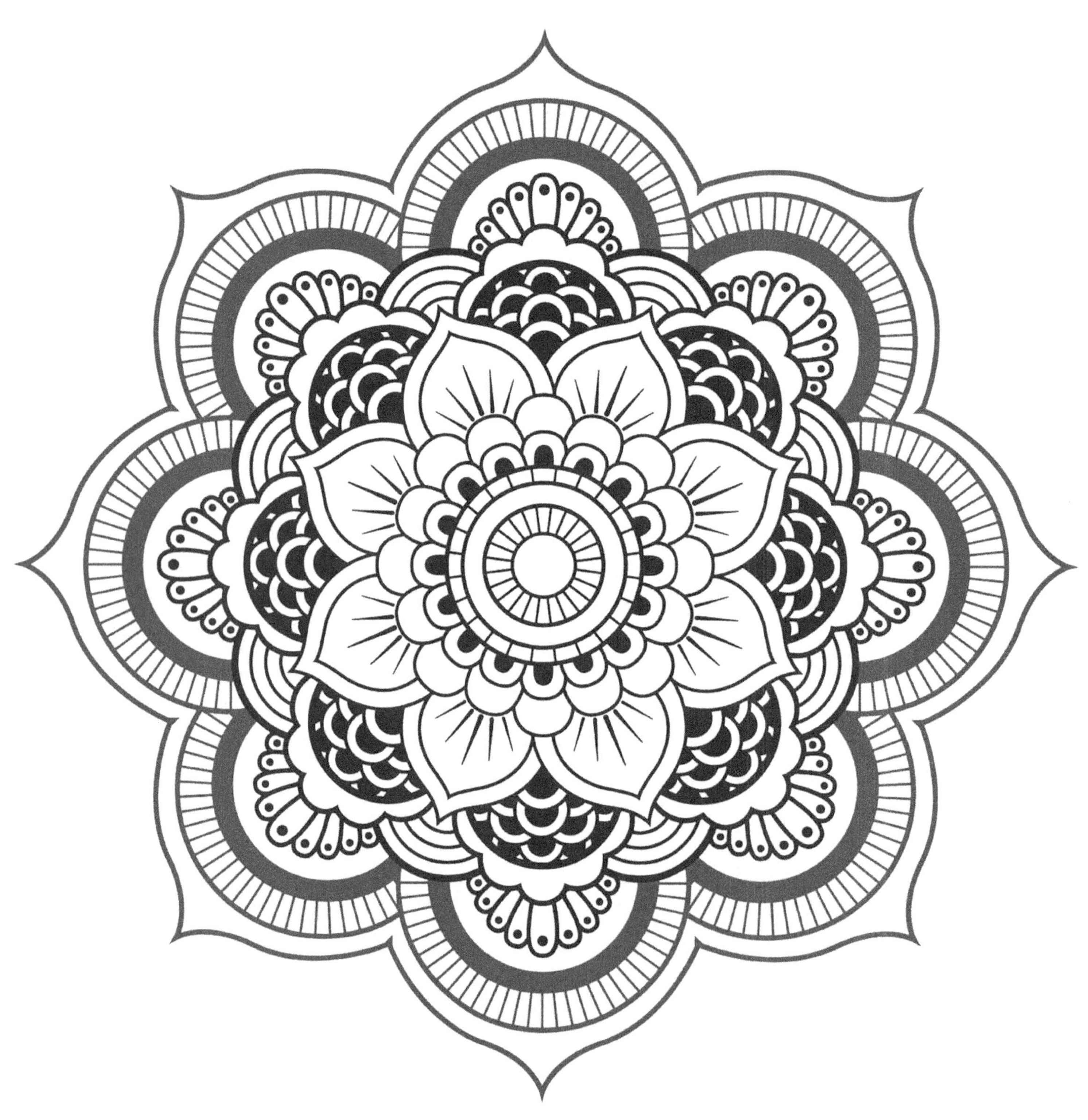

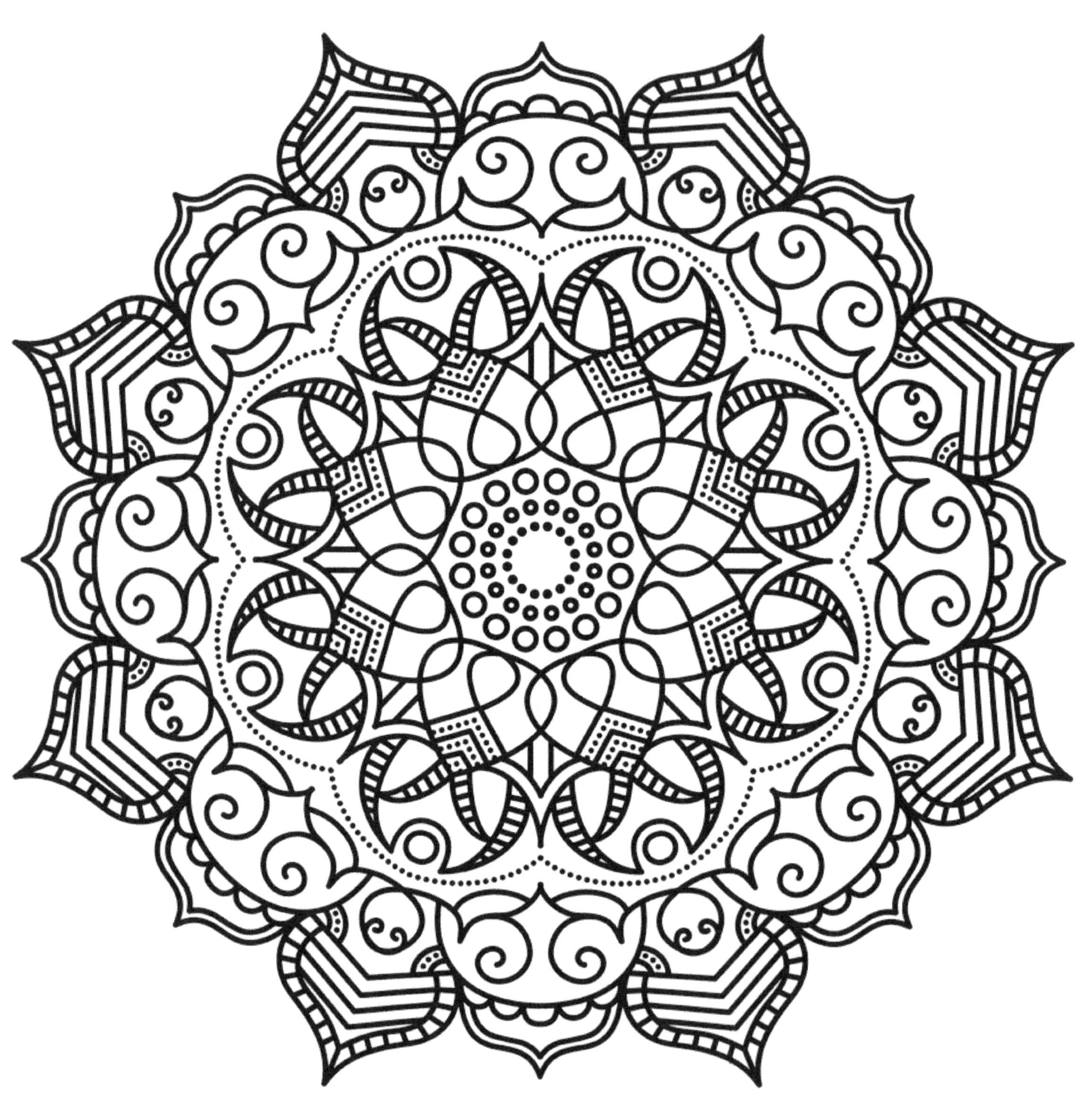

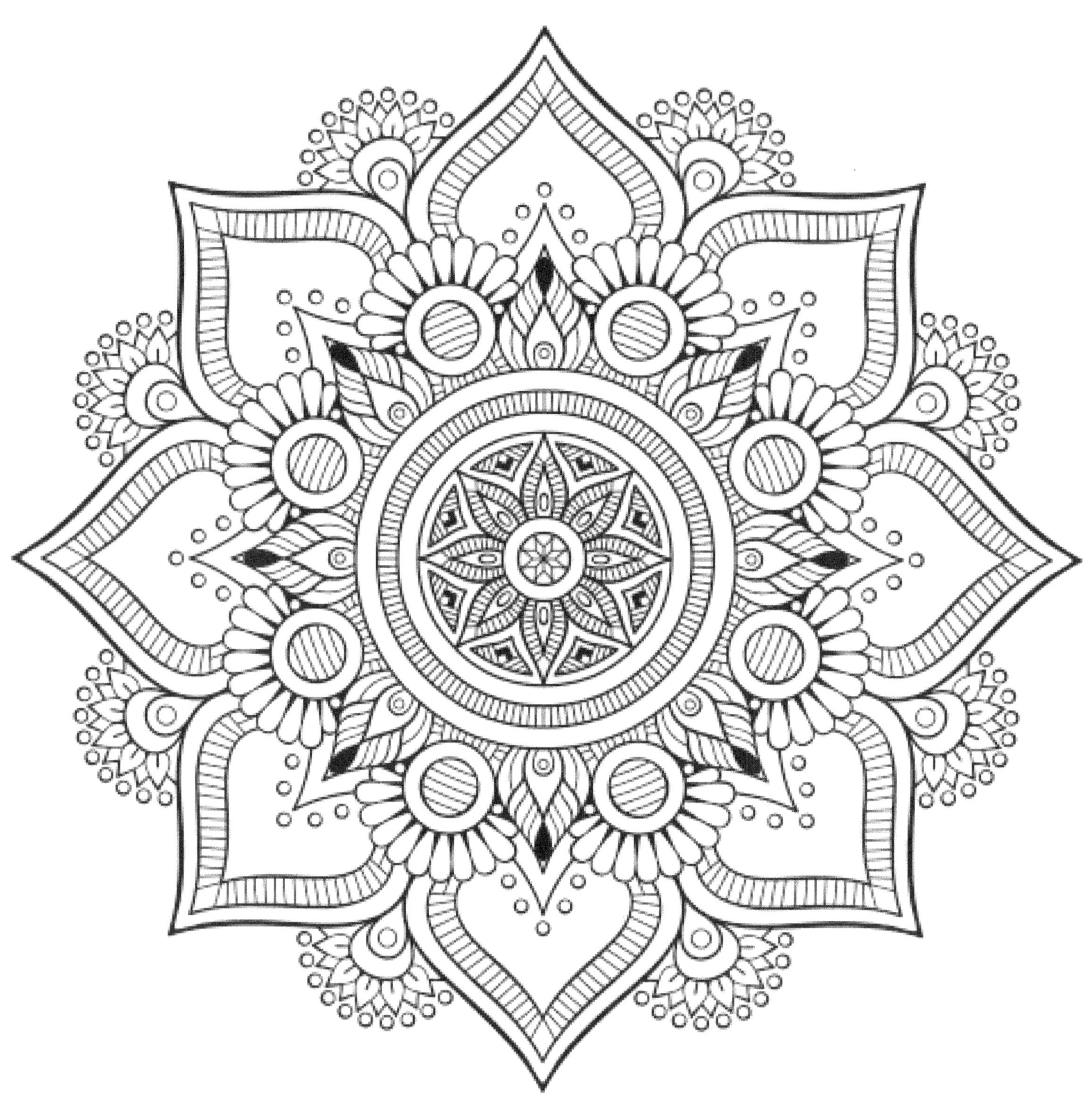

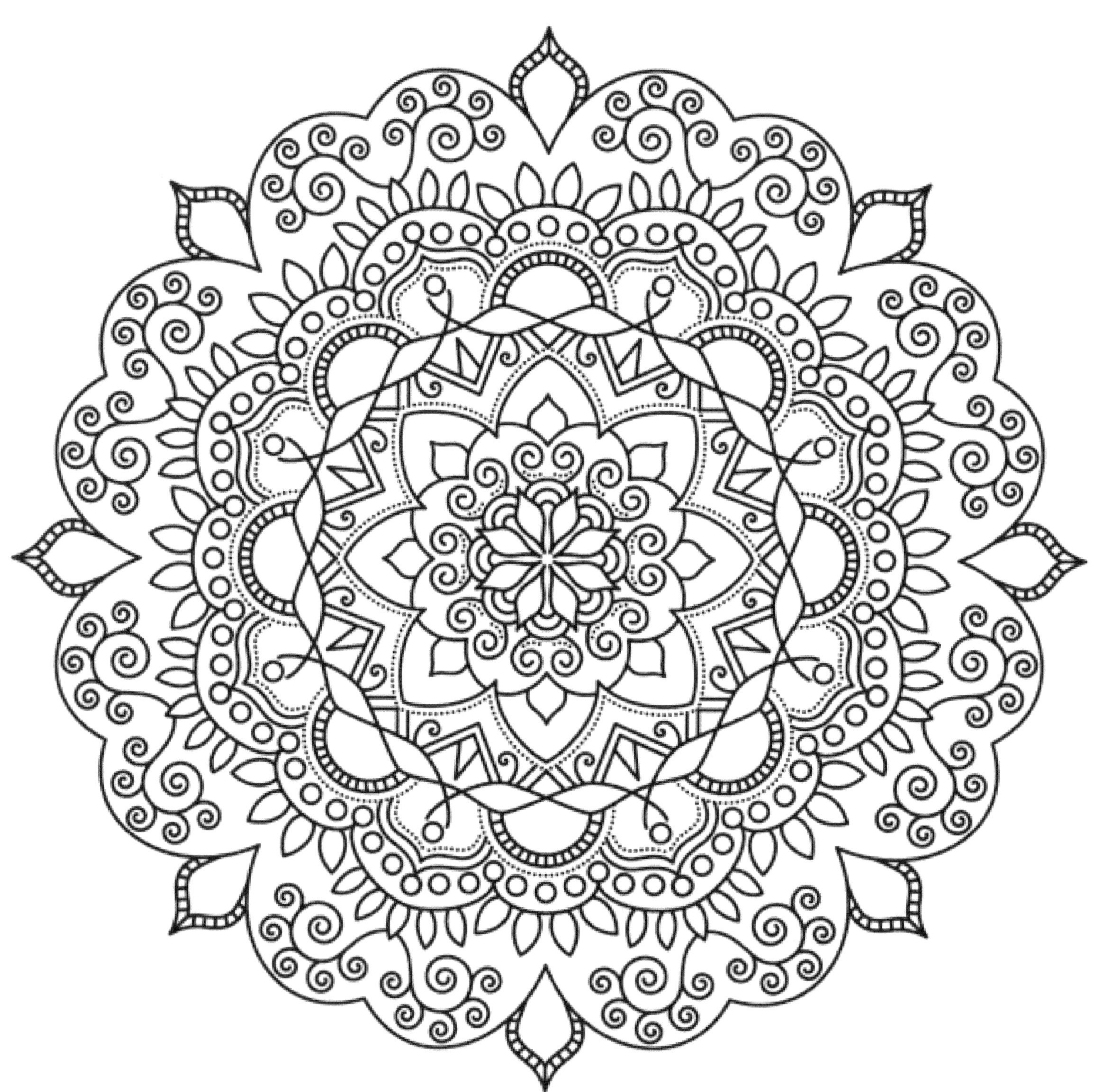

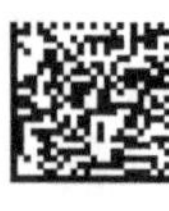

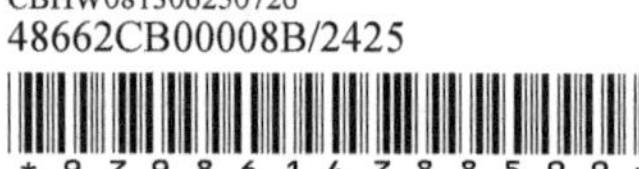